CW00501835

TAME THE FLAME
COOKBOOK

RECIPES TO REDUCE CHRONIC INFLAMMATION

MELINDA KEEN

Copyright © 2019 Melinda Keen

Editor: Jessica Matthews

All rights reserved. No part of this book may be reproduced by any mechanical or electronic process nor copied for public or private use other than for "fair use" as brief quotations embodied in articles and reviews without prior written permission.

Disclaimer:
The author of this book does not dispense medical advice or prescribe the use of any techniques as a form of treatment for physical, emotional, or medical problems without the advice of a physician, either directly or indirectly. The intent of the author is only to offer information of general nature to help you in your quest for emotional, physical, and spiritual well-being. A heath care professional should be consulted regarding your specific situation.

ISBN: 9781094687568

CONTENTS

INTRODUCTION

Food has a profound impact on health. It is important to eat a wide variety of foods from the five food groups to ensure that you are consuming all the different nutrients that your body needs. The nutrients in food enables the cells in our bodies to perform their necessary functions. We especially need to pay attention to what we eat when we are ill so we can give our bodies the nutrients it needs to heal. The processed, low-variety foods many of us consume regularly may be convenient and tasty, but they have been shown to compromise our health. Processed food includes food that has been canned, packaged, or changed in nutritional composition with fortifying, preserving, or preparing in different ways. Many contain additives and high amounts of added sugar and sodium. Research indicates that there is a link between the foods you consume and inflammation.

Eating healthy is not about strict limitations, staying unrealistically thin, or eliminating food groups. We are often told that staying fit, maintaining a healthy weight, and improving health requires a diet. The list of diets and their various rules and restrictions, is endless. Most of them are not sustainable and are unhealthy in the long run. Every food group has important nutrients, vitamins and minerals that your body needs. Meats, grains, fruits, vegetables, and dairy all work together to help regulate the body's inflammatory process. Cutting out one of these five food groups could cause an unhealthy level of inflammation. Even when diagnosed with a food allergy there are other options within that food group. The most common food allergies are milk, eggs, tree nuts, peanuts, soy, shellfish and wheat. It may appear that a whole food group must be eliminated for one of these allergies but there are often replacements within that food group. A milk allergy doesn't mean a dairy allergy. A common replacement for a milk allergy is goat milk. The same principle applies with a wheat allergy. Other options within the grain food group include oats, cornmeal, and wild rice.

Sometimes foods touted as superfoods have damaging effects. They contain a high volume of minerals, vitamins, and antioxidants, but they are not cure all foods. For example, overeating kale can interfere with thyroid function, chia seeds can inhibit the absorption of certain minerals, and excess intake of spinach can lead to kidney stones and joint pain. Including superfoods as part of daily nutritional intake is great but only when consuming an overall healthy, balanced diet. Health as well as weight loss occurs on its own when you start making better food choices. It also involves removing foods that cause inflammation and adding a variety of foods that are anti-inflammatory. You don't have to be perfect, you don't have to completely eliminate foods you enjoy, and you don't have to change everything all at once. The best approach is to make a few small changes at a time. Cooking more meals at home can help you take charge of what you're eating and better monitor what goes into your food. You'll avoid the chemical additives, added sugar, and unhealthy fats of packaged and takeout foods. The recipes in this cookbook are easy to follow; high in key vitamins and minerals, protein, and fiber; and are catered to individuals with food sensitivities and are dealing with chronic inflammation.

The Flame That Fans Disease

Inflammation is an immune response of body tissues to injury or infection. The course of events that occur during an inflammatory response can vary. White blood cells, blood, proteins, and fluids rush to the affected site to destroy the irritant and flush it from the body, often causing swelling, redness, pain, and heat. These white blood cells, blood, proteins, and fluids can repair damage, stop the spread of infection or illness, and in some cases eradicate the intruder. This type of Inflammation, called acute inflammation, starts rapidly, becomes severe in a short time, and symptoms may last for a few days or weeks. Without inflammation your body would be defenseless when faced with an injury or illness. It's a healthy and necessary function for healing. When the infection or illness is gone, inflammation should go away as well. When this doesn't happen, and the response lingers leaving your body in a constant state of alert, it can result in chronic or long-term inflammation. Chronic inflammation can last for months or even years. Food allergies, intolerances, and toxic food substances are often a source of chronic inflammation.

Chronic inflammation often begins with something irritating your body and stimulating your immune system. It comes on slowly as a result of a stressor such as an allergy, food intolerance, or a toxic food substance. The body's natural immune response goes awry. Low levels of inflammation can get triggered in the body even when there's no disease to fight or injury to heal, and sometimes the system can't shut itself off. It can affect any and all parts of the body. White blood cells swarm but have nothing to do and nowhere to go, and they may eventually start attacking internal organs or other healthy tissues and cells. Over time, chronic inflammation will have a negative impact on your tissues and organs. The problem with chronic inflammation is that it's often hard to diagnose and manage.

Chronic inflammation can result from any number of reasons. Anything your immune system perceives as an attack elicits an inflammatory response. Every cell in your body is affected by chronic inflammation. Compromised cellular function results in oxidative stress, DNA damage, and toxic overload. Over time, chronic inflammation opens you up to compromised health. Increased inflammation makes it easier for normal cells to transform into malignant cells. Many people experience the symptoms of chronic inflammation daily, without actually realizing what is causing it. Aches and pains are the results of the immune system attacking the tendons and ligaments that make up our joints. Another common form of out of control inflammation can be found in the gut. Gut inflammation symptoms might directly feel like pain, bloating, or gas, and this can indirectly affect many different parts of the body. Immune cells stay active and on the attack until the source of inflammation is addressed and healing begins.

Inflammation and immune imbalances are at the root of most of modern disease. Several things can cause chronic inflammation, including an infection or injury or long-term exposure to irritants, such as industrial chemicals or polluted air, smoking, and alcohol. Lack of sleep, not enough physical activity, and chronic stress are also believed to largely affect the level of inflammation in the body.

Lifestyle choices and diet play a role in the conditions brought about by chronic inflammation. In the following pages you will learn about food intolerances, foods that are known to cause inflammation, foods that are known to be anti-inflammatory, and how to reduce inflammation naturally to improve your overall health. The recipes to reduce chronic inflammation contain plenty of prebiotics, fiber, antioxidants, and omega-3s. A natural, less processed diet rich in vegetables, whole fruits, legumes, and fatty fish can have noticeable effects on your health.

Signs and symptoms of chronic inflammation include fatigue, body aches, joint pains, fibromyalgia, gastrointestinal issues, hypertension, sleep problems, weight gain (especially belly fat), headaches, and puffiness in the face or hands. Eventually, chronic inflammation results in several diseases and conditions including rheumatoid arthritis, cancer, heart disease, diabetes, and even Alzheimer's.

Diet is one of the major factors. There are some foods known for their pro-inflammatory effects. Food allergies, food intolerances, and toxic food substances are often a source of chronic inflammation. Researchers believe that by changing your diet by eating healthy, reducing pro-inflammatory foods, identifying your own food intolerance or allergy, and removing those foods from your diet will reduce chronic inflammation in your body.

Inflammatory Sparks

A diet high in pro-inflammatory foods, food allergies, and food sensitivities or intolerances are the leading sources of chronic inflammation. Knowing the sources that spark inflammation can help you adjust your diet to keep your body from over-producing inflammatory chemicals. Although toxic effects from foods vary from person to person, some foods are pro-inflammatory to most people. These include sugar, refined carbs, and highly processed foods.

Some of the symptoms of food allergy and a food intolerance are similar, but the differences between the two are very important. A true food allergy causes an immune system reaction that affects many organs in the body. In some cases, an allergic food reaction can be severe or life-threatening. In contrast, food intolerance symptoms are generally less serious and often limited to digestive problems. Hidden food sensitivities or intolerances can inflame the gut, activate an immune response, and cause system-wide chronic inflammation. Because they are sometimes less obvious and can take up to 72 hours to develop, food sensitivities may remain unrecognized in many people. I recommend an elimination diet to help identify food sensitivities. An elimination diet is divided into two phases: elimination and reintroduction. Eliminate a food that you suspect your body might not be tolerating well for at least two weeks. If your symptoms still remain after removing the food for two weeks, eliminate a different food and repeat. Each time slowly reintroduce the food you eliminated. If you experience negative symptoms, then you have successfully identified a trigger food and should remove it from your diet.

Inflammatory Foods

What we eat may help prevent and keep chronic inflammation in check. A healthy eating plan provides nutrients that help keep your immune system working well. Research has linked excess consumption of certain foods to higher inflammation. Were you to eat these foods on occasion, chronic inflammation probably wouldn't happen as a result of your diet. Were you to eat these foods frequently or in excess, the chances of inflammation are much higher. Research suggests that processed meats, trans fats, and refined carbs and sugars promote chronic inflammation. Eating high amounts of processed meat over a long period may increase the risk of many chronic diseases, such as heart disease and cancer. Processed meat contains many harmful chemicals that are not present in fresh meat. Ingestion of processed meat is associated with an increase in the inflammatory marker CRP (C-reactive protein).

When food manufacturers transform vegetable oils into solids, by a process called hydrogenation, trans fats are created. For the sake of texture and preservation, trans fats show up in most margarines, shortening, and foods cooked with partially hydrogenated oils. Trans fat can also increase inflammation in your body and contribute to blocked arteries and heart disease by damaging your blood vessels. Fast food is among the worst trans-fat offenders. Most cooking oils go through an insane amount of processing with chemical solvents, steamers, neutralizers, de-waxers, bleach and deodorizers before they end up in the bottle. Soy and canola oil, as well as less familiar products like corn, peanut, sunflower, safflower, and cottonseed oil, all fall under the term of "vegetable oils." This makes them sound a lot healthier than they really are. Margarine is made from vegetable oil, so it also falls in this category. Because vegetable oils oxidize easily, they deplete the body of antioxidants as they attempt to neutralize the oxidation. People with high consumption of vegetable oils are at risk for Vitamin E deficiency and other deficiencies. These oils are known to be toxic to the liver, compromise the immune system, increase levels of uric acid in the blood, and have been known to cause inflammation and mutation in cells. Excess consumption of polyunsaturated oil is associated with increasing rates of cancer, heart disease, and weight gain. While it is simple enough to avoid these oils themselves, the tougher challenge is avoiding all the foods they are in. Check out practically any processed food, and you will find at least one of these oils. Most deep-fried foods in restaurants are fried in either soybean or canola oil. Fast food is high in trans fats, sugar, and sodium as well as processed preservatives and ingredients. A lot of well-conducted research has proven the negative health effects of consuming too much of these.

Refined or processed carbs have had most of the nutrients and fiber removed. Refined carbs include mostly processed grains and sugars. They are empty calories and lead to rapid spikes in blood sugar and insulin levels. Table sugar (sucrose) and high-fructose corn syrup (HFCS) are the two main types of added sugar in the Western diet. Consuming a diet high in sugar and high-fructose corn syrup drives inflammation that can lead to disease. If you care about your health, then it is crucial to keep high fructose corn syrup out of your diet. High fructose corn syrup is a sweetener made from corn starch. High fructose corn syrup is most commonly found in soda, but it is also found in cereal, juice, and many store-bought desserts. Staying away from this sweetener will cut your risk of diabetes, weight gain, inflammation, and even certain cancers.

Your body cannot process artificial ingredients well, so substances such as aspartame and monosodium glutamate may trigger an immune response. Aspartame is a neurotoxin that the body frequently "attacks" thereby causing inflammation. Artificial ingredients are often hidden in processed food, condiments, and spice mixes. Aspartame in particular is commonly found in soft drinks, especially "diet" or "healthier" beverages. It may be hard to avoid, but sugar is one of the leading causes of inflammation. Sugar causes the release of inflammatory proteins known as cytokines. While these proteins are important in fighting against inflammation, there are both pro and anti-inflammatory cytokines, and sugar releases the pro-inflammation variety.

Inflammatory Foods List

Processed meats (sausage, bacon, ham, smoked meat, beef jerky, deli meats)
Trans Fats (partially hydrogenated oils, margarine, shortening)
Refined Carbohydrates (candy, cereals, cookies, cakes, doughnuts, breads)
High fructose corn syrup
Sugar
Soft drinks
Artificial sweeteners
Soybean oil

Corn oil
Safflower oil
Canola oil
Peanut oil
Cottonseed oil
Deep-fried restaurant meals
Fast Foods

Allergies

Food allergies illicit an abnormal immune response that triggers an immediate or delayed hypersensitivity reaction. Histamine is released, causing varying degrees of symptoms like lightheadedness; itching; hives or rash; swelling of the lips, tongue, and throat; nausea; vomiting; and diarrhea. Rarely, a food allergy will trigger a life-threatening, whole-body reaction known as anaphylaxis in which airways constrict and blood pressure drops swiftly causing shock, loss of consciousness, and sometimes death. An allergy is the immune system's overreaction to a normally harmless substance. People with food allergies must avoid the dietary culprit. The top food allergies are milk, eggs, tree nuts, peanuts, wheat, soy and seafood. Sometimes it can be difficult to tell food allergies and food intolerances apart. If you suspect you have a food allergy, it's important to speak to your doctor to find out whether you have an allergy or an intolerance. Your doctor will probably carry out a number of diagnostic tests. Food intolerance symptoms are generally less serious and often limited to digestive problems and inflammation. If you have a food intolerance, you may be able to eat small amounts of the offending food without trouble. For example, if you have lactose intolerance, you may be able to drink lactose-free milk or take lactase enzyme pills (Lactaid) to aid digestion, but if you have a milk allergy you must avoid all milk products. Due to the number of possible food allergies it is impossible to address and label these recipes for each one.

Gluten

Celiac disease is a serious, genetic autoimmune disorder triggered by consuming a protein called gluten. Gluten is a protein composite found in wheat and related grains, including barley and rye. It causes inflammation in the small intestine of people with celiac disease. For the person reeling under a doctor's directions to avoid gluten, the task of creating family friendly nourishing meals can be overwhelming. Eating gluten-free may sound restrictive, but the recipes in this cookbook prove it doesn't have to be boring or complicated.

If you have been suffering from symptoms that seem related to gluten but your blood test for celiac disease was negative, it may be possible that you have non-celiac gluten intolerance or allergy. An important difference between gluten intolerance and wheat allergy is that the symptoms of gluten intolerance are not deadly, whereas a wheat allergy can potentially be life-threatening. The symptoms of wheat allergy include nausea and vomiting, diarrhea, mouth or throat irritation, rash, hives or difficulty breathing. People experiencing this should call an ambulance immediately. It is important to get medical advice urgently for a suspected wheat allergy as severe allergic reactions can quickly threaten life.

Symptoms of gluten intolerance include belly pain and bloating, which occurs after eating foods that contain gluten. Common foods that contain wheat and gluten include breads, pastas, wheat-based crackers, and certain seasonings and spice mixes. Most of the recipes in this cookbook are gluten free and are identified as such.

Gluten Foods List

Bulgur
Couscous
Wheat
Barley
Malt Vinegar
Brewer's Yeast

Lectins

Lectins are naturally occurring proteins that are found in most plants. They serve a protective function for plants as they grow. Studies have shown that lectins break down when processed or cooked, so the risk of adverse health effects arising from lectin-rich foods that aren't raw is not cause for concern. Cooking, especially with wet high-heat methods like boiling or stewing, or soaking in water for several hours, can inactivate most lectins. Lectins are water-soluble and typically found on the outer surface of a food, so exposure to water removes them. Most foods that contain lectins are recommended as part of a healthy, well-balanced diet. The body can produce enzymes during digestion that also degrades some lectins.

Lectins can act as an antioxidant, which protects cells from damage caused by free radicals. They also slow down digestion and the absorption of carbohydrates, which may prevent sharp rises in blood sugar and high insulin levels. Lectin-rich foods include whole grains, nuts, beans, tomatoes, onions, eggplants, and bell peppers. For some people, eating lectins poses a health concern. Lectin rich foods are often listed in the top food allergens. People with food allergies must avoid the dietary culprit. An intolerance or sensitivity to lectins may show up as symptoms such as fatigue, rashes, joint pain, nausea and gut discomfort. If you suspect a food intolerance, I recommend trying the elimination diet to identify the dietary culprit instead of eliminating all foods that contain lectins.

Lectin Foods List

Beans
Legumes
Peas
Lentils
Chickpeas
Peanuts
Squash
Eggplant
Peppers
Potatoes
Tomatoes
Grains

Oxalates

Oxalates cannot be seen, tasted, or smelled yet people consume them almost every day. A healthy human body has the ability to manage mild levels of oxalates in foods. Some are degraded by the oxalate-degrading anaerobic bacterium that colonizes the large intestines and some are bound by minerals during digestion and are excreted. If the body isn't able to process oxalates in this manner, they have a negative impact on your health. Oxalates, also called oxalic acid, are naturally occurring substances found in varying degrees primarily in plant foods such as vegetables, fruits, grains, legumes, spices, herbs, and almost all nuts and seeds. These molecules are present in the leaves, roots, stems, fruits and seeds. Some foods, such as rhubarb, spinach, and raspberries have especially high levels. Oxalates in foods are classified as antinutrients meaning they interfere with the absorption of vitamins, minerals, and other nutrients. They even get in the way of digestive enzymes, which are vital for proper digestion and absorption of nutrients.

Generally, a healthy individual will not experience ill effects from small amounts of oxalates in the diet. Most people are able to safely metabolize a certain amount of oxalates in foods due to specific bacteria in the digestive tract called Oxalobacter formigenes, or safely pass them as they bind with minerals like magnesium and calcium. Problems occur when gastrointestinal microbiota has been reduced or depleted and ingested oxalates are not metabolized. Oxalates that are not safely metabolized or bound by minerals in the gastrointestinal tract and excreted are then absorbed through the gastrointestinal barrier and enter the bloodstream. The key site for problems with accumulation of oxalates in the bloodstream is the kidneys. High oxalates in the kidneys tend to combine with calcium to form calcium oxalate stones, the most common type of kidney stone. High oxalates elsewhere in the bloodstream tends to bind with essential elements such as calcium, magnesium, iron and copper and end up deposited in body tissues causing damage and exacerbating pain and inflammation. The most common location is in the joint or connective tissues, but these crystal deposits have also been found in the heart, brain, and even in the bones.

There are several factors that may explain why oxalates are not able to be eliminated and pass into the bloodstream. Oxalate rich foods are tolerated by most people as long as they are not eaten in excess or consistently over long periods of time. In excessive amounts, oxalates can build up in the blood and urine with extremely toxic results. A lack of normal digestive bacteria, as found with chronic candida, can lead to increased oxalate availability and absorption into the blood. The gastrointestinal tract is home to microbes that are capable of degrading oxalates, but unfortunately, many commonly used antibiotics can kill these oxalate degrading microbes. If gastrointestinal bacteria has been compromised either by alcohol consumption, yeast overgrowth, poor diet, or antibiotic use, oxalates will not be degraded. The body will respond with protective measures such as binding the oxalate with minerals. Some people are unaware of oxalate accumulation until they have reached their own tipping point and symptoms arise. These powerful and very reactive molecules can wreak havoc on your health. Varied effects of high oxalates in cells and tissues interferes with and damages mitochondrial function, thereby impairing cellular energy, creates oxidative stress, results in digestive issues, damages tissues, and causes histamine release. This in turn can trigger widely varied symptoms, including fatigue, joint pain, or pain anywhere in the body. Oxalates can be a hidden source of headaches, urinary pain, genital irritation, and joint, muscle, intestinal, or eye pain. Calcium oxalate crystal arthritis can result from deposit of calcium oxalate crystals within bones, tendons, cartilage or the fluid in the joints of the shoulder, elbow, wrist, knee, or ankle. A deposit in a tendon can cause it to bulge and become inflamed. An inflamed tendon between bones make it difficult and painful to move. Calcium oxalate crystal arthritis sometimes called pseudo-gout, may be more painful and severe than most osteoarthritis. Other common oxalate-caused symptoms may include mood conditions, anxiety, sleep problems, weakness, or burning feet. Many of the problems caused by oxalates go misdiagnosed because they are easily associated with aging. It's also easy to assume that certain problems are the result of better known causes that create similar symptoms.

If you are not finding relief through your doctor it's quite possible your condition is oxalate related. An "oxalate-free" diet is impossible. Oxalates occur in varying amounts in almost all plant foods. If you eat food, you're almost certainly consuming oxalates in some amount. Typical diets contain upward of 200–300 mg of oxalate, but you can lower your oxalate load to less than 50 mg of oxalate per day. This is usually recommended for individuals that have a history of kidney stones or increased levels of oxalic acid in their urine. Withdrawing from oxalate rich foods, even for as short as two weeks, can determine whether oxalate influence is at the root of your health problems. All of the recipes in this cookbook have low oxalate ingredients and are marked as such.

High Oxalate Foods List

Rhubarb
Beets
Okra
Eggplant
Parsnip
Rutabaga
Spinach

Yams
Sweet potato
All beans
Dates
Kiwi
Orange
Raspberries
Figs
Prunes
Brown Rice
Corn Grits
Millet
Soy Flour
Tofu
Sesame seeds
Pecans
Almonds (including almond milk and flour)
Cashews
Peanuts
Pistachios
Walnuts
Chocolate
Cocoa Powder
Black Tea

Nightshades

Nightshades are members of the family Solanaceae. Common nightshades include white (but not sweet) potatoes, eggplants, tomatoes, and peppers, both the eye-watering chilies and the sweeter bell peppers. The list of edible nightshade plants also includes any spices made from peppers, like paprika, red pepper flakes, and cayenne pepper. Most people have no problems with nightshades. Some people simply have a digestive sensitivity or intolerance to nightshades. Nightshade vegetables can act as a trigger similar to wheat or dairy and cause major inflammation and immune reactions to some people. If you aren't sensitive to them, there's absolutely no reason to rush out and eliminate these foods. Meanwhile, a true nightshade allergy, like any food allergy, should be taken seriously. However, it may not be easy to pinpoint. While many allergens are easy to single out, nightshade vegetables are not associated with one another. If you are exhibiting signs of a food allergy it's important to speak to your doctor for diagnostic tests. Nightshade vegetables should be considered in an elimination diet if you suspect a digestive sensitivity or intolerance to nightshades.

Nightshade Foods List

Tomatoes
Tomatillos
Bell peppers
Eggplant
White potatoes
Chili peppers
Cayenne pepper
Paprika
Goji berries

Reducing Chronic Inflammation

Currently, there are no prescription drugs that specifically targets chronic inflammation. There are, of course, over-the-counter medications that treat the minor and temporary inflammatory pain. These are not meant to treat chronic inflammation long term. Some of the conventional treatment options include over-the-counter nonsteroidal anti-inflammatory drugs (NSAIDs), such as aspirin, ibuprofen (Advil and Motrin), naproxen (Aleve) and acetaminophen (Tylenol). However, long-term use is linked to an increased risk of several conditions, including peptic ulcer and kidney disease.

Corticosteroids, such as cortisone and prednisone, are often prescribed as chronic inflammation treatment for conditions like arthritis and asthma. They decrease inflammation and suppress the immune system, which is helpful when it starts attacking healthy tissue. Side effects of oral corticosteroids used on a short-term basis include fluid retention, increased appetite, weight gain, insomnia, and mood changes. Side effects of oral corticosteroids used on a long-term basis (for more than three months) include osteoporosis, high blood pressure, diabetes, weight gain, increased vulnerability to infection, cataracts, glaucoma, muscle weakness, thinning of the skin, and bruising easily.

I personally wouldn't recommend any of the conventional options for long-term use. I encourage caution with dietary supplements touted as anti-inflammatory cures. Some so-called inflammatory remedies, such as turmeric, taken in large amounts may actually be toxic to the liver and other organs. Instead, opt for natural remedies that really get to the root of the problem.

Your food choices have the biggest impact on health. Removing the food sources of chronic inflammation such as inflammatory foods, food intolerances, and toxic food substances will naturally reduce chronic inflammation. Replacing these foods with more whole natural foods, such as fruits, vegetables, lean proteins, natural healthy fats, and anti-inflammatory foods, will have a profound effect on your health. Eating such a diet may restrict where you eat, so cooking at home will likely become a necessity. It doesn't mean you have to spend hours in the kitchen combining dozens of different ingredients or following elaborate recipes. In fact, simple meals are often the tastiest. This cookbook is filled with delicious recipes that are high in key vitamins and minerals, are additive free, and are natural foods that will reduce chronic inflammation.

I believe that choosing foods that are as close to their natural state as possible is the key to a long healthy life. Another key part of a healthy diet is the absence of toxic chemicals. We should be eating foods that will nourish the body like clean, real, pesticide and hormone free products. This means cutting out processed foods and replacing them with natural whole foods such as dairy, fruits, vegetables, herbs, meats, and eggs. Replacing processed food with real food, preferably organic, whenever possible makes a huge impact on health. Herbicides and pesticides used on crops remain on fruits and vegetables even after they are washed. USDA resources found a total of 178 different pesticides and pesticide breakdown products on the thousands of produce samples they had analyzed. There is no legal limit on the number of different pesticides allowed on food, and the effects of these chemicals are unknown. Because synthetic chemicals are not allowed on organic foods, eating organic is one of the best ways to lower your overall toxic burden.

Conventionally raised meat sources are often given drugs and hormones to grow faster, as well as antibiotics. Their diets are based on corn and soy, usually treated with pesticides, which are not the animal's natural diet. In the U.S., the majority of both corn and soy are genetically modified. Organic meats and eggs reduce your exposure to hormones, antibiotics, and pesticides. Growth hormones and antibiotics are prohibited under organic regulations. Grass-fed cows, wild-caught fish, and pasture-raised poultry eat a natural diet free of pesticides and genetic modification. Lessening this toxic burden gives the body a chance to detoxify and reset health. Our bodies constantly require nutrients to function and must be supplied with wholesome food for optimal performance and health. Supplying your body with good nutrition gives your body the building materials to restore health.

Meat, Fish, and Eggs

For optimal health I choose grass-fed organic beef and lamb, pasture-raised turkey and chicken, wild-caught fish, and pasture-raised organic eggs. In order to be certified to the US Department of Agriculture's (USDA) organic standards, farms and ranches must follow a strict set of guidelines. The animals' organic feed cannot be grown using pesticides or chemical fertilizers, be genetically engineered, or contain animal by-products or antibiotics. No antibiotics or added growth hormones are allowed to be given to the animals and they must have outdoor access. If you prefer to replace some of the meats with pork, I highly recommend you find a naturally raised, pastured source. Pork can have a lot of contaminants, including the controversial drug ractopamine, which is banned in many parts of the world. Farm-raised fish commonly contains high levels of contaminants as well.

Farmed fish are fed an unnatural diet of grains and legumes. The healthiest choice is wild-caught fish. These fish tend to be higher in Omega 3 fatty acids, contain very low levels of disease, and are free from antibiotics and pesticides. Omega-3 fats found in salmon and other wild-caught, cold-water fish, as well as grass-fed beef and dairy, have been shown to reduce muscle, bone, and joint pain by lowering inflammation. Studies show that a lower ratio of omega-6s to omega-3s can reduce the risk of many chronic diseases.

Protein is important for repair, maintenance, and growth of cells and is essential for healthy muscles, organs, glands, and skin. Consuming a moderate amount of protein by eating beef, fish, and poultry, and eggs can provide high-quality protein. Plant based foods high in protein as well as fiber include lima beans, pumpkin seeds, broccoli, avocados, and Brussels sprouts.

Grains

Most of my recipes do not include whole grain wheat as it is high in oxalates and a common gluten sensitivity or allergenic food. White rice is a gluten-free grain that is low in oxalates, so I add rice to my meals on occasion. Plain cornmeal, oats, and wild rice are gluten-free whole grains. Choosing organic guarantees these grains are not genetically modified. Genetically modified grains are engineered to withstand high amounts of herbicide and to produce their own internal insecticide. With health on the line, it's best to err on the side of caution and stick with organic.

Carbohydrates in grains provide the body with energy and are a good source of many vitamins and minerals. They are considered the body's most preferred source of energy for all metabolic functions. Oats and wild rice are high in fiber. Dietary fiber is a type of carbohydrate that the body can't digest. It adds bulk to your diet, makes you feel full faster, helps digestion, and helps prevent constipation. Approximately 50% of the energy obtained by the foods we eat are derived from carbohydrates and the remaining 50% is derived from proteins and fats.

Fruits and Vegetables

It is best to eat fruits and vegetables grown organically, but if budget or availability restricts your choice, remove outer leaves or peels and wash thoroughly. Organic growers are prohibited from using synthetic pesticides that have harmful effects on your health. Buy fresh and ripe fruits and vegetables when they are in season. Otherwise choose frozen. Frozen produce is processed at peak ripeness and is the most nutrient-packed aside from fresh. My recipes rarely include canned vegetables. My main concern is their sodium content, as sodium is often added to help maintain the flavor of vegetables during the canning process. When I do use them, it's usually because I can't find them fresh or frozen, I rinse them well in a colander. At times, I do choose food in jars, such as jams, simply to save time. Buying an organic product is important for health and nutrition.

Fruits and vegetables contain a variety of nutrients including vitamins, minerals and antioxidants. Vegetables are rich in vitamin A, vitamin C, folate, fiber, and potassium.

Dairy

Regardless of whether you opt for raw, organic lightly pasteurized, or organic pasteurized, the full-fat version is the healthier choice. When the fat is removed from milk, what remains are a significant number of fat-soluble vitamins that can't be absorbed as well as an overabundance of lactose.

Dairy provides calcium and vitamin D as well as protein and other essential nutrients such as phosphorus, potassium, magnesium, and vitamins A, B12, and riboflavin. The calcium in milk is easily absorbed and used in the body, which is why milk and dairy foods are reliable as well as economical sources of calcium. Cultured dairy foods like yogurt contain probiotics which provide a wide array of health benefits. Probiotics in the diet can enhance the good bacteria in the gut, improve health, and reduce the risk of certain diseases

Herbs, Spices and Salt

Beyond adding flavor, herbs and spices carry unique antioxidants, phytosterols, and many other nutrient substances that help our body fight germs and boosts the immune system. Fresh herbs are more readily available during the summer months, especially if you grow your own, but some do better when they are dried. Basically, fresh herbs and spices are added near the end of a dish, and dried ones are best added during the cooking so the flavor has time to infuse the whole dish. It is best to choose organic herbs and spices due to the fact that these are plants that are conventionally grown with the use of pesticides. Pepper comes from the fruit of the pepper plant. The peppercorns are processed two different ways. Black peppercorns are sun-dried to turn the pepper black. To produce white pepper, the outer layer is removed leaving only the inner seed. The high oxalate content of black pepper comes from the outer layer of the peppercorn. Therefore, white pepper is low in oxalate content and preferred in all of my recipes. If you prefer, small amounts of black pepper can be used in these recipes.

Sea salt and table salt have the same basic nutritional value. I use sea salt or pink Himalayan salt in my recipes because table salt is more heavily processed to eliminate minerals and usually contains an additive to prevent clumping.

Fats

Eating healthy, high-quality fat is crucial. Most of my recipes are made with grass-fed cow's milk butter, ghee, organic unrefined coconut oil, and extra-virgin olive oil. Butter, especially from grass-fed cows, is a natural healthy alternative to unnatural and harmful hydrogenated vegetable oils, margarines and shortenings, or genetically modified oils. Coconut oil is the healthiest fat for frying and sautéing because it can withstand high heat without chemically altering. Unrefined coconut oil has the flavor of fresh coconuts since it is not deodorized or chemically processed. It is rich in proteins, vitamins, and antioxidants. Extra-virgin olive oil is a healthy fat to include in your diet if it's not overheated. It should never be used as a hot frying oil but can be used in pan frying at a lower temperature. If the oil is truly extra-virgin it has a distinctive taste and is loaded with antioxidants, some of which have powerful health benefits.

Anti-Inflammatory Foods List

Avocado
Broccoli
Kale
Peppers
Mushrooms
Extra-virgin olive oil
Olives
Coconut
Cherries
Salmon
Mackerel
Sardines
Dark leafy greens such as Kale and Collards
Cauliflower
Red Wine (in moderation)
Apples
Berries
Nuts
Garlic
Onions
Squash
Sweet Potatoes

Recipes To Reduce Chronic Inflammation

Breakfasts, Brunches, and Breads

AVOCADO BANANA SMOOTHIE

Creamy, fruity, and deliciously tasty smoothie that is loaded with healthy fat and protein.

SERVES 2
INGREDIENTS

1 avocado
½ cup plain whole milk yogurt
1 banana
2 tablespoons honey
6 ice cubes

1. In a blender, combine all ingredients.
2. Blend until smooth and serve.

COOK'S NOTE

Full of fiber and healthy fats, avocado makes this smoothie creamy, dreamy and thick, almost like a milkshake.

NUTRITIONAL INFORMATION
Calories 315 Carbohydrate 42g Fat 16.9 Protein 5g

CHERRY VANILLA SMOOTHIE

Naturally sweet frozen cherries and coconut milk blend to make a cold, creamy, delicious and refreshing smoothie.

SERVES 2
INGREDIENTS

1 ½ cups frozen pitted cherries, frozen
1 ¼ cups coconut milk
½ teaspoon vanilla extract

1 cup water

1. Place the cherries, milk, vanilla extract, and water in the blender and blend until smooth.
2. Pour the smoothie into 2 glasses and serve.

COOK'S NOTE
Cherries are a potent source of antioxidants and anti-inflammatory compounds. Coconuts contain a lipid called lauric acid, and many researchers believe that lauric acid can support the immune system. Combining these in this smoothie gives you a powerful health boost to start your day.

NUTRITIONAL INFORMATION
Calories 521 Carbohydrate 52g Fat 36g Protein 6g

CUCUMBER CANTALOUPE SMOOTHIE
A light and refreshing smoothie.

SERVES 2
INGREDIENTS

1.5 ounces romaine
1 cucumber
1 cup cantaloupe
Juice of ½ lemon
1 cup water
½ cup ice cubes

1. Place all ingredients in blender and blend until smooth.
2. Serve.

COOK'S NOTE
Stay hydrated with cucumbers and cantaloupe, both contain 96 and 90 percent water.

NUTRITIONAL INFORMATION
Calories 75 Carbohydrate 11g Fat 3g Protein 3g

TROPICAL SMOOTHIE
Quick, easy, naturally sweet, tasty and gluten-free.

SERVES 2
INGREDIENTS

1 cup coconut milk
1 large banana
1 cup mango
1 cup pineapple

1. Place the coconut milk, banana, mango, and pineapple in a blender and blend until completely smooth.
2. Pour the smoothie into 2 glasses and serve.

COOK'S NOTE
When mango and pineapple are out of season you can often find them in the freezer section.

NUTRITIONAL INFORMATION
Calories 518 Carbohydrate 107g Fat 9.3g Protein 12g

AVOCADO AND CREAM CHEESE OMELET
The warm, creamy combination of avocado and cream cheese enhances the flavor of the egg in this luscious omelet.

SERVES 2
INGREDIENTS

2 eggs
1 tablespoon whole milk
¼ teaspoon salt
2 tablespoons butter, 1 tablespoon per omelet
½ medium avocado, chopped
1 ounce cream cheese, chopped
Paprika (as desired)

1. In a mixing bowl, whisk together the egg, milk, and salt.
2. Melt 1 tablespoon butter in a 10 or 12 inch skillet over medium heat.

3. Pour half of the egg mixture in the skillet and spread it out evenly around the bottom by rotating the skillet. Cook until done.
4. Sprinkle half of the avocado and half of the cream cheese over one half of the egg.
5. Fold the other half of the egg over the top of the avocado and cream cheese.
6. Allow the cheese a few seconds to melt; then transfer to a plate.
7. Repeat the process for the second omelet.
8. Sprinkle with paprika and serve.

COOK'S NOTE
The healthy, beneficial fats make this a blood sugar balancing breakfast.

NUTRITIONAL INFORMATION
Calories 296 Carbohydrate 6g Fat 28g Protein 8g

EGG AND CHEESE TOSTADA
An easy recipe made with soft fried eggs, tomato, and cheddar cheese layered on top of crisp tortillas.

SERVES 2
INGREDIENTS

2 6-inch corn tortillas
2 large egg, fried
2 tablespoons roma tomatoes, diced
2 tablespoons cheddar cheese, shredded

1. Preheat oven to 350 degrees.
2. Bake tortillas on oven rack for 8 to 10 minutes or until crisp.
3. Top each with fried egg, tomato, and cheese.

COOK'S NOTE
To be sure this recipe is gluten-free look for certified gluten-free corn tortillas.

NUTRITIONAL INFORMATION
Calories 493 Carbohydrate 67g Fat 18.3g Protein 18g

SALAD OMELET

A light and refreshing vegetarian omelet with a garden fresh salad between the folds.

SERVES 2
INGREDIENTS

3 eggs
1 tablespoon whole milk
1 tablespoon onion, minced
1 tablespoon red or yellow bell pepper, minced
¼ cup cheddar cheese, shredded
1 tablespoon butter
½ cup lettuce, shredded
½ cup tomatoes, diced
Salt and pepper (as desired)

1. In a large mixing bowl, whisk the eggs.
2. Add in milk, onion, pepper, and cheese. Mix well.
3. In a large nonstick skillet, heat the butter over medium-high heat.
4. Pour the egg mix in the skillet and rotate the skillet to spread the mixture out evenly.
5. Lower the heat to medium and cook without stirring until almost done; then remove from heat.
6. Slide the egg to a plate and add the lettuce and tomato to one half of the egg; then fold the other half over the top.
7. Salt and pepper as desired; slice in half and serve.

COOK'S NOTE

This recipe makes a delicious light lunch or dinner as well. Each serving provides 22% of your daily requirements for vitamin K and 19% of your daily requirement for vitamin B12.

NUTRITIONAL INFORMATION
Calories 273 Carbohydrate 4g Fat 22g Protein 16g

YOGURT PANCAKES

Easy, delicious, grain free and protein rich pancakes.

SERVES 2
INGREDIENTS

½ cup coconut flour
¼ teaspoon baking soda
¼ teaspoon salt
4 eggs, beaten
1 tablespoon butter, melted
1 tablespoon honey
½ teaspoon vanilla
½ cup plain whole milk yogurt
3 tablespoons water
Coconut oil or ghee (for frying)
Maple syrup (as desired)

1. In a medium-size bowl, mix the coconut flour, baking soda, and salt together.
2. In a separate bowl, beat the eggs, then add the butter, honey, vanilla, yogurt, and water.
3. Pour the egg mixture over the coconut flour and mix well. Allow the mix to sit a minute or two to thicken.
4. In a large skillet, heat a small amount of coconut oil or ghee over medium heat.
5. Pour palm size cakes and shake the skillet a bit to spread them out without touching each other. (In a large skillet you can cook 2 or 3 at a time.)
6. Cook about 2-3 minutes until bubbly on top, and then turn. Cook an additional 2 minutes or until golden brown.
7. Serve hot with maple syrup.

COOK'S NOTE
These fluffy and filling pancakes need to be cooked slowly over medium heat. The recipe can easily be doubled or tripled.

NUTRITIONAL INFORMATION
Calories 614 Carbohydrate 25g Fat 53g Protein 17g

AVOCADO TOMATO TOSTADA

Creamy avocado sits atop a crisp baked tostada for a fresh and flavorful meal.

SERVES 4
INGREDIENTS

4 6-inch corn tortillas
2 avocados, peeled and mashed
¼ teaspoon salt
1 garlic clove, minced
1 cup roma tomato, chopped
Lemon juice, as desired

1. Preheat oven to 350 degrees.
2. Bake tortillas on oven rack for 8 to 10 minutes or until crisp.
3. In a medium-size bowl, peel and mash the avocados with the salt and garlic.
4. Remove the crisp tortillas and top each with the avocado and tomato.
5. Squeeze a small amount of lemon juice over each and serve.

COOK'S NOTE

Tostada means "toasted" in Spanish and is typically used as the base ingredient of a dish. Corn tortillas used in this recipe are lightly toasted in the oven and become the base for all the healthy toppings.

NUTRITIONAL INFORMATION
Calories 235   Carbohydrate 24g   Fat 15.7g   Protein 4g

AVOCADO AND CHEESE TOSTADA

Creamy avocado sits atop a crisp baked tostada with a cheese topping.

SERVES 4
INGREDIENTS

4 6-inch corn tortillas
2 avocados, peeled and mashed
¼ teaspoon salt
1 garlic clove, minced
1 cup cheddar cheese, shredded
Lemon juice, as desired

1. Preheat oven to 350 degrees.
2. Bake tortillas on oven rack for 8 to 10 minutes or until crisp.
3. In a medium-size bowl, peel and mash the avocados with the salt, garlic, and lemon juice as desired.
4. Remove the crisp tortillas and top each with the avocado and cheese.

COOK'S NOTE
You can also toast the corn tortillas with the cheese on top then top with the avocado.

NUTRITIONAL INFORMATION
Calories 363 Carbohydrate 23g Fat 26.8g Protein 12g

CORNMEAL LOAF BREAD
A healthy and delicious loaf of bread for the gluten-free sandwich lover.

SERVES 8
INGREDIENTS

3 eggs, beaten
1 tablespoon maple syrup
2 cups whole milk
2 cups cornmeal, plain
1 ½ teaspoons salt
1 teaspoon baking soda
2 tablespoons butter, melted

1. Preheat oven to 400 degrees.
2. In a small bowl; beat the eggs and add the maple syrup and milk. Mix well.
3. In a separate bowl, combine the cornmeal, salt, and baking soda.
4. Add the wet ingredients to the dry and pour in the melted butter. Mix until smooth.
5. Oil a 6x9 loaf pan and pour in ingredients.
6. Bake for 40 minutes and allow to cool before slicing.

COOK'S NOTE
Unlike ordinary cornbread this loaf slices well making it perfect for a healthy whole grain sandwich bread.

NUTRITIONAL INFORMATION
Calories 238 Carbohydrate 37g Fat 7g Protein 7g

AVOCADO EGG BAKE

A fast, healthy, and nutritious breakfast of warm soft avocado and creamy egg.

SERVES 2
INGREDIENTS

2 large avocados, ripe but firm
4 eggs, the smaller the better
½ teaspoon salt
¼ teaspoon pepper

1. Preheat oven to 450 degrees.
2. Line a small baking dish with parchment paper. Look for a small baking dish that would allow the avocado halves to stand upright.
3. Cut the avocados in half lengthwise and remove the pits. Using a spoon, scoop out a little of the flesh of each avocado and season with half of the salt and pepper.
4. Place them in the prepared baking dish.
5. Break each egg into a small bowl. Then carefully slide the yolk and as much as will fit of the white into the center of each avocado half.
6. Bake until whites are set. (About 15 minutes.)
7. Season the baked avocado egg with the remaining salt and pepper and serve.

COOK'S NOTE

Beyond the heart-healthy fatty acids and high protein count, this low-sugar and fiber-filled breakfast will kick off your day on a healthy high note.

NUTRITIONAL INFORMATION
Calories 208 Carbohydrate 8g Fat 17g Protein 7g

SALMON SCRAMBLE

A classic combination of creamy scrambled eggs and chunks of buttery salmon.

SERVES 4-6
INGREDIENTS

5 eggs
1 tablespoon milk or cream
¼ teaspoon salt
⅛ teaspoon white pepper
1 tablespoon fresh chopped chives
2 tablespoons butter
1 can (14 ounces) wild-caught Alaskan salmon, drained
¼ teaspoon dried dill

1. In a medium-size mixing bowl, combine the egg, milk, salt, pepper, and chives. Blend well.
2. In a large nonstick skillet, heat the butter over medium heat, and pour in the egg mixture.
3. Stir eggs until almost set then gently stir in and break up salmon and add the dill.
4. Continue to cook until salmon is warmed, and the eggs are set.
5. Serve hot.

COOK'S NOTE

This quick and easy, low-carbohydrate, protein and omega-3 rich breakfast will satisfy the heartiest appetite. Each serving supplies 64% of your daily requirement for vitamin B12 and 44% of your daily requirement for vitamin B6.

NUTRITIONAL INFORMATION
Calories 270 Carbohydrate 1g Fat 17g Protein 27g

SAUSAGE PATTIES

A simple recipe for making your own classic, tasty sausage patties.

SERVES 6
INGREDIENTS

1 pound ground turkey, grass fed-beef, bison or venison
1 tablespoon white wine vinegar
1 teaspoon onion powder
½ teaspoon mustard seed
½ teaspoon sage
½ teaspoon rosemary
¼ teaspoon salt
½ teaspoon cayenne pepper
½ teaspoon white pepper
½ teaspoon garlic powder
¼ teaspoon cumin
¼ teaspoon chili powder
¼ teaspoon fennel
2 tablespoons coconut oil or ghee (for frying)

1. In a large mixing bowl, combine all of the ingredients and mix well.
2. Form patties and cook in an oiled skillet over medium-high heat until golden brown on both sides. (Makes 12 patties.)
3. Serve hot.

COOK'S NOTE
Say goodbye to all those food additives and make your own sausage. You'll never go back to buying ready-made again.

NUTRITIONAL INFORMATION
Calories 160 Carbohydrate 1g Fat 11g Protein 14g

SAUSAGE CASSEROLE

An easy and incredibly delicious breakfast for dinner meal.

SERVES 4
INGREDIENTS

1 pound ground turkey (grass fed-beef is another option)

1 tablespoon Dijon mustard
½ teaspoon sage
½ teaspoon rosemary
¼ teaspoon salt
½ teaspoon cayenne pepper
½ teaspoon white pepper
½ teaspoon garlic powder
¼ teaspoon cumin
¼ teaspoon chili powder
¼ teaspoon fennel
½ medium red onion, diced
1 medium zucchini, shredded.
5 eggs
1 ½ cup Italian blend shredded cheese
Butter, enough to lightly oil casserole dish

1. Preheat oven to 375 degrees.
2. In a large mixing bowl combine the ground turkey, mustard, sage, rosemary, salt, cayenne pepper, white pepper, garlic powder, cumin, chili powder and fennel to make the sausage. Mix well.
3. In a large skillet sauté the sausage and onion over high heat until browned.
4. Add the zucchini and cook a minute more.
5. In a separate mixing bowl beat the eggs and stir in the cheese.
6. Mix the eggs and cheese with the browned sausage and pour into a lightly buttered 9x13 casserole dish.
7. Bake for 20 minutes.
8. Cool for 5 minutes before serving.

COOK'S NOTE
Say goodbye to all those food additives and make your own turkey sausage. You'll never go back to buying ready-made again. The sausage can also be made into patties or sausage balls.

NUTRITIONAL INFORMATION
Calories 587 Carbohydrate 5g Fat 41g Protein 49g

BAKED MUSHROOM FRITTATA

A simple and flavorsome oven-baked Italian frittata with mushrooms, scallions, and parmesan cheese.

SERVES 4
INGREDIENTS

1 tablespoon olive oil
16 ounces baby bella mushrooms, sliced
8 large eggs
¼ cup plain whole milk yogurt or sour cream
¼ teaspoon sea salt
¼ teaspoon white pepper
¼ teaspoon dried thyme
½ cup scallions, chopped
½ cup parmesan cheese, grated

1. Preheat oven to 400 degrees.
2. Place a 9-inch pie dish in the oven to warm it up.
3. Heat the olive oil in a large skillet over medium heat. Add the mushrooms. Cook the mushrooms until browned and tender and all liquids have evaporated, about 10 minutes.
4. In a medium sized bowl beat the eggs with the yogurt, salt, pepper and thyme.
5. Add the scallions and the cheese, mixing them in with a spatula.
6. Remove the warm pie dish from the oven and brush in a little olive oil to coat the dish.
7. Transfer the mushrooms to the baking dish. Then pour the egg mixture on top.
8. Return the baking dish to the oven and bake about 30 minutes until edges are brown, frittata is golden brown and puffy, and a knife inserted in the center comes out clean.
9. Allow to cool for about 10 minutes. Then slice into eight triangles and serve.

COOK'S NOTE
Mushrooms are very low in calories and rich in selenium, copper and all of the B vitamins. They also contain phenols and other antioxidants that provide anti-inflammatory protection.

NUTRITIONAL INFORMATION
Calories 274 Carbohydrate 6g Fat 18g Protein 23g

SALMON CAESAR SALAD

This salmon Caesar salad is a healthy and delicious take on a classic Caesar salad.

SERVES 2
INGREDIENTS

Dressing:
2 garlic cloves, minced
¼ cup olive oil
1 tablespoon white wine vinegar
1 egg
½ cup parmesan cheese, shredded or grated

Salad:
3 cups romaine lettuce, chopped
1 can (6 ounces) wild-caught Alaskan salmon, chopped

1. Add the garlic, olive oil, vinegar, egg and cheese to a blender and puree until smooth.
2. Divide the romaine lettuce onto 2 plates.
3. Top the lettuce with salmon and pour the dressing over each salad.

COOK'S NOTE
You can replace the canned salmon with either fresh cooked salmon you've cooked just for the occasion, or with leftover filets.

NUTRITIONAL INFORMATION
Calories 523 Carbohydrate 7g Fat 42.4 Protein 28g

AVOCADO TOMATO SALAD

A simple summer salad with the flavorful combination of tomato and avocado.

SERVES 4
INGREDIENTS

2 cups tomato, chopped
½ cup cucumber, chopped
2 tablespoons red onion, diced
2 tablespoons olive oil
2 teaspoons balsamic vinegar
¼ teaspoon salt
3 garlic cloves, minced
1 teaspoon dried basil
½ cup black olives, sliced
2 avocados, peeled and chopped

1. In a large mixing bowl, add all of the ingredients except the avocado and mix well.
2. Add the avocado and gently mix.
3. Let stand for about 5 minutes, and gently mix again before serving.

COOK'S NOTE

A slight tweak on the traditional Greek salad introduces the rich and creamy texture of avocado as a replacement for lettuce and feta cheese. The many health benefits of avocado have made it a popular addition to any dish. This dish is an omega-3 powerhouse.

NUTRITIONAL INFORMATION
Calories 279 Carbohydrate 16g Fat 25g Protein 3g

VEGETABLE EGG STIR-FRY

This blend of fresh vegetables with eggs is delicious over shredded romaine lettuce for a meal in minutes.

SERVES 2-4
INGREDIENTS

1 cup romaine, shredded

1 small red onion, chopped
½ red pepper, chopped
2 tablespoons butter
½ bunch (10-15 spears) asparagus, tough ends trimmed and cut into 1 inch pieces
⅓ cup water
1 medium zucchini, shredded
5 eggs, beaten
1 small tomato, chopped
1 avocado, peeled and chopped
½ cup cheddar cheese, shredded
Cayenne pepper (optional)

1. Divide the shredded romaine onto 2 plates.
2. In a large skillet over medium-high heat stir-fry the onion and pepper in the butter until soft.
3. Add the asparagus and water. Cook the asparagus about 3 minutes.
4. Add the shredded zucchini and cook an additional 2-3 minutes.
5. Pour in the beaten eggs and stir often until cooked soft.
6. Remove from heat and spoon over romaine lettuce.
7. Add the chopped tomato and avocado.
8. Top with cheese and cayenne pepper.

COOK'S NOTE
Eggs contain high quality proteins, fats, vitamins and minerals. Pair them with vegetables for a powerful combination of antioxidant nutrients.

NUTRITIONAL INFORMATION
Calories 698 Carbohydrate 39g Fat 50g Protein 34g

CAULIFLOWER MOCK POLENTA WITH EGG
A corn-free take on polenta using cauliflower.

SERVES 4
INGREDIENTS

1 large cauliflower head
4 tablespoons butter or ghee
3 cups water
¼ teaspoon salt
1 egg, cooked as desired

1. Chop the cauliflower into chunks and pulse the pieces in a food processor. Pulse until all the cauliflower is in very small grain-like pieces.
2. Add butter to a large frying pan. On medium heat add the cauliflower and half of the water.
3. Simmer for about 15 to 20 minutes, or until the cauliflower is soft. While it's simmering, add the salt and a bit more water if needed.
4. Serve warm topped with egg cooked as desired.

COOK'S NOTE
Cauliflower is considered by many to be one of the healthiest foods due to its rich supply of health-promoting phytonutrients and high level of anti-inflammatory compounds.

NUTRITIONAL INFORMATION
Calories 138 Carbohydrate 3g Fat 13g Protein 3g

GREEN PEA AND FETA TOSTADA
Peas, feta cheese and fresh mint combine in this light and flavorful dip to serve over toasted corn tortillas.

SERVES 4
INGREDIENTS

2 cups green peas, fresh or frozen
½ cup water
3 tablespoons olive oil
1 tablespoon lemon juice

1 tablespoon fresh mint, chopped
½ teaspoon salt
¼ teaspoon white pepper
8 corn tortillas
½ cup crumbled feta cheese

1. Preheat oven to 400 degrees.
2. Add the peas and ½ cup water to a saucepan. Bring to a boil, then simmer, covered, stirring occasionally, 5 to 10 minutes.
3. Drain the peas, then transfer them to an ice bath for a few minutes to stop the cooking and drain again.
4. Transfer the peas to a food processor fitted with a blade. Add 2 tablespoons of the oil, the lemon juice, mint, salt and pepper. Pulse several times, until the mixture is spreadable but retains some texture.
5. Spread the tortillas out on a large baking sheet and brush lightly with oil.
6. Bake approximately 3 min. each side.
7. Spread 2 heaping tablespoons of the pea mixture onto each tortilla and top with feta cheese.
8. Drizzle each with 1 tablespoon of the remaining olive oil.

COOK'S NOTE
This recipe can also be used as a dip, a side dish, or a salad topping.

NUTRITIONAL INFORMATION
Calories 315 Carbohydrate 35g Fat 16.1g Protein 10g

AVOCADO AND BEAN SPROUT TOSTADA

A simple vegetarian tostada with avocado and mung bean sprouts.

SERVES 4
INGREDIENTS

4 6-inch corn tortillas
2 avocados, peeled and mashed
¼ teaspoon salt
1 garlic clove, minced
1 cup mung bean sprouts
Lemon juice, as desired

1. Preheat oven to 350 degrees.
2. Bake tortillas on oven rack for 8 to 10 minutes or until crisp.
3. In a medium-size bowl, peel and mash the avocados with the salt and garlic.
4. Remove the crisp tortillas and top each with the avocado and bean sprouts.
5. Squeeze a small amount of lemon juice over each and serve.

COOK'S NOTE
This recipe can also be created without the corn tortilla. Simply add the ingredients to a bowl or top your salad and enjoy.

NUTRITIONAL INFORMATION
Calories 236 Carbohydrate 24g Fat 15.7g Protein 5g

BANANA MUFFINS

A moist and wholesome muffin with all natural ingredients.

SERVES 6
INGREDIENTS

½ cup coconut flour
½ teaspoon baking powder
1 teaspoon baking soda
½ teaspoon salt
5 eggs
1 cup banana, mashed
½ teaspoon vanilla
2 tablespoons honey
¼ cup butter, melted

1. Preheat oven to 400 degrees and oil a 12 cup muffin pan or line with paper cupcake liners.
2. In a large bowl, mix the coconut flour, baking powder, baking soda, and salt.
3. In a separate bowl, combine the eggs, mashed banana, vanilla, honey and melted butter. Whisk well.
4. Pour the egg mix over the coconut flour and mix well.
5. Fill muffin cups two-thirds to three-quarters full.
6. Bake for 14-15 minutes. Remove when they start to brown and a toothpick inserted in the center comes out clean.
7. Allow to cool about 5 minutes before transferring to a serving dish.
8. Serve warm with a pat of butter on top.

COOK'S NOTE
Choose very ripe bananas if you desire a more intense banana flavor.

NUTRITIONAL INFORMATION
Calories 298 Carbohydrate 19g Fat 23g Protein 6g

SKILLET PIZZA

A quick and easy pizza with a cheese crust instead of the usual flour crust. Top with any of your own favorite toppings.

SERVES 1
INGREDIENTS

½ cup cheddar cheese
1 roma tomato, sliced thin
2 tablespoons red onion, chopped
2 tablespoons black olives, sliced
¼ teaspoon garlic powder
¼ teaspoon dried oregano

1. Evenly sprinkle the cheese in a 10-inch nonstick skillet.
2. Heat over medium heat until the cheese has melted.
3. Top with the tomatoes, onions, and olives.
4. Sprinkle with the garlic powder and oregano.
5. Continue cooking the pizza over medium heat until the bottom and edges are browned. Be careful not to burn the cheese crust.
6. Remove the skillet from the heat. Allow about 30 seconds for it to become crisp. Then use a spatula and carefully slide it onto a cutting board.
7. Immediately cut the skillet pizza into 8 wedges.
8. Briefly place the pizza wedges on paper towels to soak up extra grease and serve.

COOK'S NOTE

It's important to cut this skillet pizza into wedges before it cools completely, because it really crisps as it cools and becomes hard to slice.

NUTRITIONAL INFORMATION
Calories 240 Total Fat 19g Carbohydrates 3g Protein 13g

CHEESE BISCUITS
A light garlic and cheddar cat-head biscuit

SERVES 4
INGREDIENTS

5 eggs, beaten
1 cup cheddar cheese, shredded
½ cup coconut flour
½ teaspoon baking powder
¼ teaspoon garlic powder
½ teaspoon salt
¼ cup butter, melted
¼ cup water
¼ teaspoon garlic powder

1. Preheat oven to 400 degrees.
2. In a mixing bowl, beat the eggs then add the shredded cheese.
3. In a second mixing bowl, combine the flour, baking powder, garlic powder and salt.
4. Pour the egg and cheese over the flour, then add the melted butter and water.
5. Mix well and set aside for 2 minutes.
6. Drop by large spoonfuls onto parchment lined baking sheet.
7. Bake for 15 minutes and set aside to cool.

COOK'S NOTE
This recipe makes 12 great tasting low carb biscuits. These savory biscuits are grain-free, gluten-free, and sugar-free.

NUTRITIONAL INFORMATION
Calories 270 Carbohydrate 2g Fat 23.2g Protein 13g

COCONUT FLOUR SANDWICH BREAD

A delicious low carb, gluten-free sandwich bread that is baked flat rather than in a loaf.

SERVES 1
INGREDIENTS

1 ½ tablespoons coconut flour
⅛ teaspoon salt
¼ teaspoon baking powder
1 egg
1 tablespoon coconut oil or butter, melted

1. Preheat oven to 350 degrees.
2. Mix coconut flour, salt, and baking powder together until combined.
3. Add egg and melted coconut oil or butter and mix well.
4. Let batter sit for a few minutes to allow the flour to absorb the liquid.
5. Scoop half the batter onto a baking pan and use a spatula to spread batter into a circle the size of a bun. Repeat using the rest of the batter.
6. Bake for 10 minutes or until golden brown.

COOK'S NOTE

Coconut flour is made from dried coconut solids ground into a very fine powder. This a completely gluten-free flour. Yet unlike a lot of gluten-free flours, it is oxalate free. It's probably the easiest flour to start with if you're new to gluten-free cooking

NUTRITIONAL INFORMATION
Calories 218 Carbohydrate 5g Fat 20g Protein 6g

COCONUT PUMPKIN BREAD

Pumpkin and coconut combine quite nicely in this sweet bread with a nutty crunch.

SERVES 8
INGREDIENTS

½ cup coconut flour
1 ½ teaspoons baking powder
¼ teaspoon salt
6 eggs
½ cup pumpkin, cooked and mashed
½ cup maple syrup
4 tablespoons butter or coconut oil, melted
½ teaspoon nutmeg
½ cup unsweetened coconut, shredded
¼ cup raw pumpkin seeds

1. Preheat the oven to 425 degrees.
2. In medium-size bowl, add the coconut flour, baking powder, and salt. Mix well and set aside.
3. In a separate mixing bowl, beat the eggs; then blend in the pumpkin, maple syrup, butter or coconut oil, and nutmeg. Mix well.
4. Pour wet ingredients into the dry ingredients and beat until smooth.
5. Stir in half of the shredded coconut and all of the pumpkin seeds.
6. Pour the mix into a well oiled 6x9 loaf pan and sprinkle the remaining coconut on top.
7. Bake for 35-40 minutes.
8. Allow to cool before slicing and serving.

COOK'S NOTE
Pumpkin is a fabulous source of fiber, potassium, and iron.

NUTRITIONAL INFORMATION
Calories 375 Carbohydrate 26g Fat 29g Protein 8g

CHEESY ZUCCHINI FLATBREAD

A delicious low carb bread substitute with garden fresh flavor.

SERVES 4
INGREDIENTS

3 medium zucchinis, grated
2 large eggs
2 cloves garlic, minced
½ teaspoon dried oregano
2 cups cheddar, shredded
½ cup parmesan, shredded or grated
½ cup rice flour
¼ teaspoon salt

1. Preheat oven to 425 degrees.
2. Line a baking sheet with parchment paper.
3. Grate zucchini and use a cheesecloth or a clean dish towel to wring excess moisture out of the zucchini.
4. Transfer zucchini to a large bowl and add the remaining ingredients.
5. Stir until completely combined.
6. Transfer the dough to prepared baking sheet and pat into a crust.
7. Bake until golden and dry, about 25 minutes.
8. Slice and serve.

COOK'S NOTE

This recipe makes a nutritious pizza crust as well.

NUTRITIONAL INFORMATION
Calories 436 Carbohydrate 20g Fat 28.8g Protein 24g

CHEESY BREADSTICKS

A simple, cheesy breadstick that is delicious whether you are gluten-free or not.

SERVES 4
INGREDIENTS

⅓ cup plus 2 tablespoons rice flour
⅓ cup plus 2 tablespoons cornmeal flour
1 teaspoon baking powder
½ teaspoon salt
3 cloves garlic, minced
1 egg, beaten
1 tablespoon olive oil
½ cup Parmigiano-Reggiano or cheddar cheese, shredded
⅔ cup water
8 ounces mozzarella cheese, shredded

1. Preheat oven to 450 degrees.
2. In a medium-size bowl, combine the rice flour, cornmeal, baking powder and salt.
3. In a separate bowl, mix the garlic, egg, olive oil, Parmigiano-Reggiano or cheddar cheese and water. Whisk well.
4. Add the wet ingredients to the dry and mix well.
5. Spread the mix over a parchment lined baking sheet and bake for 15 minutes.
6. Top the crust with the mozzarella cheese and bake a few minutes more until the cheese melts.
7. Slice and serve. Enjoy them plain or with your favorite dipping sauce.

COOK'S NOTE
The crust is crunchy on the bottom and chewy in the middle making them the perfect gluten-free bread sticks.

NUTRITIONAL INFORMATION
Calories 359 Carbohydrate 24g Fat 16g Protein 29g

GRAIN FREE DINNER ROLLS

A soft and savory grain free faux bread roll with a light texture and taste.

SERVES 6
INGREDIENTS

3 eggs, separated
⅛ teaspoon cream of tartar
½ teaspoon honey
⅛ teaspoon salt
3 ounces cream cheese

1. Heat oven to 300 degrees.
2. In a medium-size bowl, add the egg whites and cream of tartar.
3. Using an electric mixer on high, whip the egg whites until very stiff and set aside.
4. In another medium-size bowl, add the egg yolks, honey, salt, and cream cheese.
5. Using an electric mixer on high, blend until smooth.
6. Fold the egg white mixture into the yolk mixture with a spatula.
7. Spoon 6 mounds onto an oiled baking sheet.
8. Bake 25-30 minutes.
9. Cool before removing to a serving dish.

COOK'S NOTE

This light, grain free roll is so versatile. Serve it alongside any meal, or top it with anything from avocado to your favorite jam.

NUTRITIONAL INFORMATION
Calories 83 Carbohydrate 2g Fat 7g Protein 4g

TAPIOCA BUNS
A light and airy bread, with a chewy crust and cheesy flavor.

SERVES 6
INGREDIENTS

¼ cup coconut oil, butter or ghee, melted
1 ½ cups tapioca flour (also known as tapioca starch)
1 teaspoon baking powder
¼ teaspoon salt
2 cups shredded cheese (parmesan or cheddar)
2 eggs
1 tablespoon water (if needed)

1. Preheat oven to 400 degrees.
2. Melt the coconut oil, butter or ghee and set aside to cool.
3. In a large mixing bowl combine the tapioca flour, baking powder, and salt. Careful, tapioca flour is very light and can be messy.
4. Add the shredded cheese and mix well.
5. Add the eggs and the oil. Mix it well with a fork at first and then by kneading. It has to be worked really well with your hand. It may seem too dry, but you don't want it sticky. Add 1 tablespoon of water if needed to form the dough.
6. Separate the dough into 6 equal sizes then shape each into rounds almost an inch thick.
7. Place them about an inch apart on a lightly oiled baking sheet.
8. Bake 400 degrees for 11-12 minutes. They will flatten out some and turn a very light brown. If they get too brown they will be tough.
9. Cool about 5 minutes before serving.

COOK'S NOTE
Tapioca buns are a wonderful, healthy replacement for hamburger buns.

NUTRITIONAL INFORMATION
Calories 416 Carbohydrate 35g Fat 25.4g Protein 13g

SOUPS, SALADS AND DRESSINGS

ARUGULA AND CAULIFLOWER SOUP
Cauliflower combined with arugula makes a delicious, thick peppery soup.

SERVES 6
INGREDIENTS

1 tablespoon olive oil
1 onion, chopped
2 garlic cloves, chopped
1 carrot, peeled and thinly sliced
1 large head cauliflower
1 bay leaf
½ teaspoon dried thyme leaves
3 cups water
2 cups milk
2 cups arugula leaves
1 teaspoon ground cumin
½ teaspoon salt
½ teaspoon white pepper

1. Heat the oil in a large soup pot then add the onion, garlic, and carrot. Cook for about 6-8 minutes over medium heat to lightly color and soften the onion.
2. Add the roughly chopped cauliflower, bay leaf, thyme, and water to the pan. Bring to a boil, then reduce the heat to low and simmer for 15–20 minutes.
3. Add the milk and arugula, and warm through without letting the soup boil.
4. Add the cumin, salt, and pepper.
5. Process half the soup in a blender.
6. Return it to the soup pot, stir and serve.

COOK'S NOTE
Arugula is a low-calorie and low-oxalate food. A full cup of arugula contains just five calories and is high in calcium and iron.

NUTRITIONAL INFORMATION
Calories 93 Carbohydrate 9g Fat 5.2g Protein 4g

CORN CHOWDER

This thick and easy, delicious recipe is the perfect comfort food full of flavors so bold you'll want to eat this
soup all year round.

SERVES 4
INGREDIENTS

1 onion, chopped
1 red bell pepper, chopped
2 garlic cloves, minced
4 tablespoons butter or ghee
1 bag (16 ounces) frozen sweet corn
¼ cup olive oil
2 cups water
2 small potatoes, peeled and diced
2 cups bone or chicken broth
½ cup plain whole milk yogurt or heavy whipping cream
¼ cup cream cheese
Salt and pepper
4 ounces cheddar cheese, shredded

1. Stir fry the onion, bell pepper and garlic in the butter until soft. Add the frozen sweet corn and the olive oil and cook for about 3 minutes.
2. Pour ¾ of the corn into a blender, add water and blend until smooth.
3. Pour the blended corn back into the pot and add remaining ingredients.
4. Bring to a boil, and then reduce the heat to medium and simmer for about 10 minutes.
5. Add salt, pepper, and cheddar cheese to taste and serve.

COOK'S NOTE
Recent research has shown that the fibrous portion of corn can support the growth of friendly bacteria in our large intestine. It can also be transformed by these bacteria into short-chain fatty acids, which can supply energy to our intestinal cells and help lower our risk of colon cancer.

NUTRITIONAL INFORMATION
Calories 938 Carbohydrate 48g Fat 69.9g Protein 36g

CAULIFLOWER AND POTATO CREAM SOUP

A simple, smooth and creamy soup of cauliflower and potatoes that's incredibly comforting and easy to make.

SERVES 6
INGREDIENTS

2 tablespoons olive oil
½ large onion, diced
1 clove garlic, minced
4 cups vegetable or chicken broth
3 red potatoes, peeled and chopped
4 cups cauliflower, chopped
1 tablespoon salt
1 teaspoon white pepper
8 ounces cheddar cheese, shredded

1. In a large pot, bring olive oil to medium heat. Add onions and sauté 5 minutes until they become translucent. Add garlic and sauté 2 minutes more.
2. Add broth to the pot and stir.
3. Add the potatoes, cauliflower, salt, and pepper. Bring the pot to a boil, then reduce to a simmer. Cook for 20 minutes until potatoes and cauliflower are soft. Test with a fork for tenderness.
4. Remove the pot from the heat.
5. Add ½ of the soup to a blender and puree until smooth. Add it back to the pot.
6. Stir in the cheese. Serve.

COOK'S NOTE

Red potatoes are considerably lower in oxalates than white or russet potatoes and all potatoes are lower in oxalates when the skin is removed. This recipe measures approximately 20mg of oxalate making it a low oxalate soup. Adding calcium rich cheddar cheese helps to bind the oxalate as well.

NUTRITIONAL INFORMATION
Calories 219 Carbohydrates 24g Fat 10 g Protein 11g

ORIENTAL SOUP

An exotic soup with the perfect blend of sweet and spice.

SERVES 4-6
INGREDIENTS

1 tablespoon coconut oil or ghee
1 red onion, chopped
2 boneless chicken breasts, cut into small cubes
3 garlic cloves, crushed
½ teaspoon ginger
½ teaspoon salt
½ teaspoon white pepper
1 teaspoon red pepper flakes
2 teaspoons chives
2 cups chicken or bone broth
1 head napa or savoy cabbage, chopped
1 ½ cups coconut milk
1 can (8 ounces) bamboo shoots, drained and rinsed
1 can (8 ounces) sliced water chestnuts, drained and rinsed
1 can (14 ounces) bean sprouts (mung beans), drained and rinsed

1. Melt the oil in a large saucepan over high heat.
2. Add the onion and sauté until soft.
3. Add the chicken, garlic, ginger, salt, peppers, and chives and continue to stir until chicken is no longer pink inside.
4. Pour in the broth, and then add the cabbage.
5. Continue to cook over high heat for about 10 minutes, until the cabbage is tender.
6. Pour in the coconut milk, bamboo shoots, water chestnuts, and bean sprouts.
7. Let it return to a boil then reduce the heat and simmer for about 5 more minutes.
8. Transfer soup to individual soup bowls and serve hot.

COOK'S NOTE
Oriental vegetables like bamboo shoots, water chestnuts, and bean sprouts have impressive health benefits. These fiber rich vegetables are loaded with antioxidants, vitamins, and minerals that strengthen the immune system.

NUTRITIONAL INFORMATION
Calories 380 Carbohydrate 24g Fat 20g Protein 29g

SLOW COOKER SANTA FE SOUP
The signature Tex-Mex flavors really come together in this rich warm soup.

SERVES 4-6
INGREDIENTS

2 tablespoons coconut oil, olive oil or ghee
1 medium onion, diced
3 garlic cloves, minced
5 medium tomatoes, chopped
½ red or yellow bell pepper, diced
¼ cup black olives, sliced
1 cup corn
1 cup fresh or frozen black-eyed peas (if using canned be sure to rinse and drain)
1 teaspoon crushed red pepper flakes
1 tablespoon fresh cilantro, chopped
1 ½ teaspoons cumin
1 teaspoon salt
¼ teaspoon pepper
¼ teaspoon chili powder
3 cups chicken or bone broth
2 boneless chicken breasts
Cheddar cheese, shredded (as desired for topping)

1. Add all of the ingredients to the slow cooker and mix well.
2. Cook on low for 8-10 hours or on high for 4-6 hours.
3. Before serving use forks to pull apart the chicken breasts. Mix well.
4. Serve in individual soup bowls and top with cheese as desired.

COOK'S NOTE
Black-eyed peas substitute for the typical black bean, which is high in oxalates.

NUTRITIONAL INFORMATION
Calories 500 Carbohydrate 54g Fat 13g Protein 46g

SUPERFOOD SOUP
A delicious, thick and hearty soup that is rich in flavor and nutrition.

SERVES 4
INGREDIENTS

1 tablespoon coconut oil, olive oil or ghee
1 red onion, chopped
3 garlic cloves, chopped
1 red bell pepper, chopped
1 head napa or savoy cabbage, chopped
4 cups chicken stock or bone broth
1 head fresh cauliflower florets, cut in 1 inch pieces
1 ½ cups pumpkin puree
½ teaspoon ginger
½ teaspoon cayenne
¼ teaspoon nutmeg
1 teaspoon salt
1 teaspoon white pepper
1 cup raw pumpkin seeds (optional)

1. In a large soup pot over medium-high heat, heat the oil and sauté the onions, garlic and red bell peppers for 2 minutes.
2. Add the Napa cabbage and cook for one minute, stirring constantly.
3. Add the broth and cauliflower and bring to a boil. Then reduce the heat to medium and simmer, stirring occasionally, for 25 minutes.
4. Blend in the pumpkin puree, ginger, cayenne, nutmeg, salt and pepper.
5. Serve in soup bowls topped with raw pumpkin seeds (optional).

COOK'S NOTE
This thick and creamy soup is packed with nutrition and flavor. Each serving supplies 33% of your daily requirement for vitamin B6, 32% of your daily requirement for vitamin K and 32% of your daily requirement for potassium. Topping your soup with pumpkin seeds is a great way to add zinc and vitamin E as well.

NUTRITIONAL INFORMATION
Calories 206 Carbohydrate 28g Fat 7g Protein 11g

SPLIT PEA SOUP
A deliciously simple vegetarian split pea soup made from a short list of ingredients.

SERVES 6
INGREDIENTS

1 tablespoon olive oil
1 red onion, chopped
1 teaspoon salt
2 cups dried split green peas, picked over and rinsed
5 cups water

1. Add olive oil to a big pot over med-high heat.
2. Stir in onions and salt and cook until the onions soften, just a minute or two.
3. Add the split peas and water. Bring to a boil then turn down the heat. Simmer for 20 minutes, or until the peas are cooked through but still a touch al dente.
4. Pour half of the cooked peas into a blender and puree smooth. Return it to the pot, and it's ready to serve.

COOK'S NOTE
Split peas are dried, peeled, and split in half sweet green peas. Split peas are a great source of protein and fiber. They are also rich in minerals such as magnesium, potassium and zinc.

NUTRITIONAL INFORMATION
Calories 259 Fat 3g Carbohydrates 43g Protein 16g

LOW OXALATE BEAN SOUP

A variety of colors and vibrant herbs and spices make this vegetarian soup flavorful, filling, and incredibly delicious.

SERVES 6
INGREDIENTS

1 cup dried black-eyed peas
1 cup dried split peas
5 cups water or chicken broth
1 cup frozen baby lima beans
1 red onion, chopped
2 garlic cloves, minced
½ teaspoon cumin
1 teaspoon oregano
½ teaspoon white pepper
1 teaspoon salt

1. Sort and rinse peas and beans with cold water. Place in a large saucepan and add water or broth.
2. Bring to a boil; then add all of the remaining ingredients except the salt.
3. Reduce heat, cover, and simmer for 3 hours or until peas are tender.
4. Add salt and serve.

COOK'S NOTE

An advantage to this bean soup recipe is that split peas, black-eyed peas, and lima beans do not have to be soaked. Lima beans are an excellent source of dietary fiber, copper and manganese. They are also a good source of folate, phosphorus, protein, potassium, vitamin B1, iron, magnesium and vitamin B6.

NUTRITIONAL INFORMATION
Calories 477 Carbohydrate 31g Fat 14.4g Protein 53g

CHICKEN CAESAR SALAD

Transform the classic Caesar into a main-course salad by topping it with seared chicken breasts, parmesan, and a fresh, bold, easy homemade Caesar dressing.

SERVES 2
INGREDIENTS

2 tablespoons coconut oil, olive oil or ghee
2 boneless chicken breasts
1 large bunch romaine lettuce, chopped
Parmesan cheese (as topping)
Dressing:
3 garlic cloves
¼ cup olive oil
¼ teaspoon Worcestershire sauce
2 tablespoons white wine vinegar
1 egg
1 teaspoon dry mustard
¼ cup parmesan, grated
¼ teaspoon white pepper
4 anchovies

1. In a non-stick frying pan, heat oil over medium-high heat and place the chicken in the hot oil. Cook for 4 minutes on each side.
2. Check if it's cooked by poking the tip of a sharp knife into the thickest part; there should be no sign of pink and juices will run clear. Set aside.
3. Place all of the dressing ingredients in a blender and blend until smooth.
4. Divide the romaine lettuce into 2 large bowls and pour equal amounts of dressing over each and toss to coat the leaves.
5. Place sliced chicken breasts on top of lettuce and garnish with parmesan.

COOK'S NOTE

Bottled dressings today seem to be loaded with genetically modified soybean oil and high fructose corn syrup, which are two of the most harmful ingredients in foods. Once you've tried this Caesar dressing recipe you will never buy bottled Caesar dressing again.

NUTRITIONAL INFORMATION
Calories 777 Carbohydrate 15g Fat 54.7g Protein 60g

CUCUMBER AND RADISH SALAD

The cool sweetness of the cucumbers balances the warm spiciness of the radishes perfectly in this fresh and fast salad.

SERVES 2
INGREDIENTS

½ cup white vinegar
1 tablespoon olive oil
1 tablespoon honey
½ teaspoon dried or fresh dill weed
½ teaspoon salt
½ teaspoon white pepper
1 cup cucumber, washed and sliced
1 cup radishes, washed and sliced

1. In a large bowl, whisk together the white vinegar, olive oil, honey, dill weed, salt and pepper.
2. Add cucumbers and radishes.
3. Stir well to evenly coat vegetables. Serve immediately or cover and refrigerate before serving.

COOK'S NOTE

Not only do radishes add some zip to your favorite salad but they are also a great source of vitamin B6 and magnesium.

NUTRITIONAL INFORMATION
Calories 126 Carbohydrate 14g Fat 6.9g Protein 1g

ARUGULA GREEK SALAD

A Greek-inspired chopped salad featuring arugula, cucumbers, tomato, olives with a light and fresh dressing.

SERVES 4
INGREDIENTS

4 cups arugula
2 small cucumbers, diced
1 roma tomato, chopped
1 cup black olives, sliced
½ medium red onion, diced
1 red bell pepper, diced
1 container (8-ounces) Feta cheese, crumbled

Dressing:
¼ cup olive oil
¼ cup white wine vinegar
½ teaspoon garlic powder
½ teaspoon dried basil
½ teaspoon dried oregano
½ teaspoon onion powder
1 teaspoon Dijon mustard
salt and pepper to taste

1. Assemble arugula, cucumbers, tomatoes, olives, onion, pepper and half of Feta cheese in a large bowl.
2. To make the dressing, add all dressing ingredients and mix well.
3. Pour about half of the dressing over the salad and toss.
4. Top with remaining Feta cheese and serve with additional dressing on the side.

COOK'S NOTE

Greek salad is a twist on a traditional tossed green salad that usually includes feta cheese, olives, cucumber, red onion and olive oil. The inclusion of these additional ingredients is a healthy way to punch up the nutrition of your salad with key vitamins and minerals.

NUTRITIONAL INFORMATION
Calories 345 Carbohydrate 11g Fat 29.6 Protein 10g

VEGETABLE PASTA SALAD

An easy, cold and colorful vegetable pasta salad.

SERVES 4
INGREDIENTS

8 ounces pasta, cooked
6 tablespoons plain whole milk yogurt or sour cream
¼ cup butter, melted
1 garlic clove, finely minced
2 tablespoons finely diced red onion
¼ teaspoon salt
¼ teaspoon pepper
¼ teaspoon dill
1 cup baby arugula, chopped
1 cup frozen peas
1 cup frozen corn

1. Cook the pasta as directed on the box.
2. Meanwhile, whisk together the yogurt, butter, garlic, onion, salt, pepper and dill in a large bowl.
3. One minute before the pasta is finished cooking to al dente, add the arugula, peas, and corn to the water.
4. Drain the pasta and vegetables in a large colander and rinse with cold water until completely cooled. If it's still hot, it will absorb too much of the dressing.)
5. Shake off as much of the excess water as possible while it's in the colander.
6. Add the drained and cooled pasta and vegetables to the bowl with the dressing.
7. Toss and serve or store in the refrigerator for up to four days.

COOK'S NOTE
The ratio of pasta to vegetables in this pasta salad is pretty even making it a wonderfully healthy salad with a blend of fiber, vitamins, minerals, enzymes, and all-around-goodness.

NUTRITIONAL INFORMATION
Calories 254 Carbohydrate 30g Fat 13.4g Protein 5g

GREEK SALAD

A Greek-inspired chopped salad featuring cucumbers, tomato, and olives with a light and fresh dressing.

SERVES 4
INGREDIENTS

2 small cucumbers, diced
1 roma tomato, chopped
1 cup black olives, sliced
½ medium red onion, diced
1 red bell pepper, diced
1 container (8-ounces) Feta cheese, crumbled

Dressing:
¼ cup olive oil
¼ cup white wine vinegar
½ teaspoon garlic powder
½ teaspoon dried basil
½ teaspoon dried oregano
½ teaspoon onion powder
Salt and pepper to taste

1. Assemble cucumbers, tomatoes, olives, onion, pepper and half of Feta cheese in a large bowl.
2. To make the dressing, add all dressing ingredients and mix well.
3. Pour about half of the dressing over the salad and toss.
4. Top with remaining Feta cheese and serve with additional dressing on the side.

COOK'S NOTE

Greek salad is a twist on a traditional tossed green salad that usually includes feta cheese, olives, cucumber, red onion and olive oil. The inclusion of these additional ingredients is a healthy way to punch up the nutrition of your salad with key vitamins and minerals.

NUTRITIONAL INFORMATION
Calories 345 Carbohydrate 11g Fat 29.6 Protein 10g

SEARED MAHI MAHI SALAD
A refreshing light meal packed with flavor and nutrition.

SERVES 2
INGREDIENTS

½ teaspoon dried basil
¼ teaspoon hot sauce (I prefer Tabasco due to the low salt content)
1 tablespoon balsamic vinegar
½ teaspoon honey
1 tablespoon olive oil
2 cups arugula
½ cup cherry or golden snack tomatoes, halved
1 large tomato, chopped
1 large radish, sliced into thin strips
1 ½ tablespoons rice flour
1 teaspoon red pepper flakes
¼ teaspoon salt
¼ teaspoon white pepper
2 tablespoons coconut olive oil or ghee
1 package (12 ounces) frozen mahi mahi fillets thawed and patted dry.

1. Blend the first 5 ingredients together for the dressing and set aside.
2. Prepare the salad ingredients and divide among plates.
3. On a large plate combine the flour, the red pepper flakes, salt and pepper.
4. Add coconut oil or ghee to a hot skillet.
5. Dredge both sides of the fish in the flour.
6. Cook fish on one side to a light golden brown, for about 3-4 minutes, then turn and cook an additional 3-4 minutes, lowering the heat to medium.
7. Place the fish in the center of each salad plate.
8. Drizzle the salad with dressing and serve immediately.

COOK'S NOTE
Fish is one of the healthiest foods you can eat. The good fat and protein have been shown to fight heart disease, boost brain health and improve skin and hair.

NUTRITIONAL INFORMATION
Calories 420 Carbohydrate 20g Fat 18g Protein 43g

MEDITERRANEAN SALAD BOWL

A satisfying one bowl breakfast, lunch or dinner of healthy vegetables and egg.

SERVES 1
INGREDIENTS

1 cup romaine, shredded
6 black olives, halved
1 avocado, chopped
¼ cucumber, chopped
1 roma tomato, chopped
2 boiled eggs, chopped
½ cup feta cheese
1 tablespoon olive oil

1. Layer the bowl in the order of ingredients.
2. Top with the crumbled feta and olive oil.

COOK'S NOTE

A super healthy and quick meal that's low in carbs and high in protein, healthy fat, and fiber.

NUTRITIONAL INFORMATION
Calories 886 Carbohydrate 30g Fat 75.9g Protein 29g

SALMON CAESAR SALAD

This salmon Caesar salad is a healthy and delicious take on a classic Caesar salad.

SERVES 2
INGREDIENTS

2 garlic cloves, minced
¼ cup olive oil
1 tablespoon white wine vinegar
1 egg
½ cup parmesan cheese, shredded or grated
3 cups romaine lettuce, chopped
1 can (6 ounces) wild-caught Alaskan salmon, chopped

1. Add the garlic, olive oil, vinegar, egg and cheese to a blender and puree until smooth.
2. Divide the romaine lettuce onto 2 plates.
3. Top the lettuce with salmon and pour the dressing over each salad.

COOK'S NOTE
You can replace the canned salmon with either fresh cooked salmon you've cooked just for the occasion, or with leftover filets.

NUTRITIONAL INFORMATION
Calories 523 Carbohydrate 7g Fat 42.4 Protein 28g

SUCCOTASH SALAD
This light lima bean and corn salad with just a drizzle of olive oil and lemon allows the flavors of the seasonal produce to shine.

SERVES 2
INGREDIENTS

1 cup frozen lima beans
1 cup frozen corn
1 tablespoon olive oil
½ red onion, diced
1 teaspoon lemon juice
¼ teaspoon salt
Pepper, as desired
1 roma tomato, chopped

1. Bring a medium-size pot of salted water to a boil. Add the lima beans and boil until just tender. (15 to 20 minutes.)
2. Add the corn, return the water to a simmer about 5 minutes then drain. Rinse under cold water to cool.
3. Meanwhile, heat 1 tablespoon olive oil in a medium-size skillet over medium-high heat. Add the onions and cook, stirring often, until tender. (About 5 minutes.) Let cool.
4. Add all of the ingredients to a bowl and toss to combine.

COOK'S NOTE
This amazing mix of summer vegetables keeps well for 2-3 days in the
refrigerator.

NUTRITIONAL INFORMATION
Calories 280 Carbohydrate 42g Fat 8.3g Protein 10g

TOMATO MOZZARELLA SALAD
Mozzarella is served with tomatoes and fresh basil and tossed with olive oil
and balsamic vinegar.

SERVES 2
INGREDIENTS

¼ cup olive oil
¼ cup fresh basil, chopped
¼ teaspoon salt
1 cup mozzarella, shredded or cubed 3 roma tomatoes, chopped
3 tablespoons Balsamic vinegar

1. Combine the oil, basil, salt, and mozzarella in a bowl.
2. Cover and let marinate for at least 20 minutes in the refrigerator.
3. When ready to serve, add the tomatoes and vinegar. Toss and serve.

COOK'S NOTE
Also called Chopped Caprese Salad, it's always better the fresher you can
serve it. This salad will stay good in the fridge for 2-3 days.

NUTRITIONAL INFORMATION
Calories 462 Carbohydrate 13g Fat 39.9g Protein 14g

PIZZA SALAD

Enjoy all the flavors of pizza in a healthy salad.

SERVES 1
INGREDIENTS

1 tablespoon olive oil
1 tablespoon white wine vinegar
½ teaspoon dried oregano
½ teaspoon salt
1 cup fresh arugula
1 cup romaine lettuce
6 leaves fresh basil torn into pieces
½ cup roma tomatoes, diced
¼ medium red bell pepper, sliced thin
¼ medium onion, sliced thin
¼ cup mushrooms, sliced
5 black olives, sliced
¼ cup mozzarella, shredded

1. To make dressing, combine oil, vinegar, oregano and salt in a small bowl; whisk to blend. Set aside.
2. Combine arugula, romaine, basil, tomatoes, bell pepper, onion, mushrooms, olives, and dressing in a large serving bowl. Mix well
3. Top with mozzarella and serve.

COOK'S NOTE
You can easily double or triple this recipe and add as many pizza toppings as you like.

NUTRITIONAL INFORMATION
Calories 194 Carbohydrate 13g Fat 12g Protein 9g

AVOCADO TOMATO SALAD

A simple summer salad with the flavorful combination of tomato and avocado.

SERVES 4
INGREDIENTS
2 cups tomato, chopped
½ cup cucumber, chopped
2 tablespoons red onion, diced
2 tablespoons olive oil
2 teaspoons balsamic vinegar
¼ teaspoon salt
3 garlic cloves, minced
1 teaspoon dried basil
½ cup black olives, sliced
2 avocados, peeled and chopped

1. In a large mixing bowl, add all of the ingredients except the avocado and mix well.
2. Add the avocado and gently mix.
3. Let stand for about 5 minutes, and gently mix again before serving.

COOK'S NOTE

A slight tweak on the traditional Greek salad introduces the rich and creamy texture of avocado as a replacement for lettuce and feta cheese. The many health benefits of avocado have made it a popular addition to any dish. This dish is an omega-3 powerhouse.

NUTRITIONAL INFORMATION
Calories 279 Carbohydrate 16g Fat 25g Protein 3g

CAESAR DRESSING

SERVES 4
INGREDIENTS

½ cup olive oil
1 egg
3 garlic cloves
2 tablespoons white wine vinegar
1 teaspoon dry mustard
1 teaspoon molasses
¼ cup parmesan cheese
4-5 anchovies
Black pepper (as desired)

1. Add all of the ingredients to a blender and process for 30 seconds until the mixture is smooth.
2. Bring to room temperature and shake or whisk well before serving. Keep refrigerated up to one week.

NUTRITIONAL INFORMATION
Calories 370 Carbohydrates 3.1g Fat 34g Protein 15.1g

HONEY MUSTARD DRESSING

SERVES 4
INGREDIENTS

½ cup mustard
¼ cup honey
¼ cup plain whole milk yogurt
1 tablespoon olive oil
1 tablespoon white wine vinegar

1. Place all of the ingredients in a jar, cover tightly, and shake.
2. Bring to room temperature and shake well before serving. Keep refrigerated up to one week.

Calories 197 Carbohydrates 25.1g Fat 9.7g Protein 5.5g

ITALIAN DRESSING

SERVES 4
INGREDIENTS

½ cup olive oil
¼ cup white wine vinegar
¼ teaspoon garlic powder
¼ teaspoon dried rosemary
¼ teaspoon dried oregano
¼ teaspoon dried basil

1. Place all of the ingredients in a jar, cover tightly, and shake.
2. Allow to sit at least 30 minutes to meld the ingredients.
3. Bring to room temperature and shake well before serving. Keep refrigerated up to 10 days.

NUTRITIONAL INFORMATION
Calories 220 Carbohydrates 0g Fat 25.2g Protein 0g

RANCH DRESSING

SERVES 4
INGREDIENTS

½ cup butter
½ teaspoon, garlic powder
½ teaspoon chives
¼ teaspoon onion powder
¼ teaspoon parsley
¼ teaspoon dill
1 cup plain whole milk yogurt

1. Melt the butter, whisk in all of the seasonings, and mix in the yogurt.
2. Allow to sit at least 20 minutes to meld the ingredients.
3. Bring to room temperature and shake well before serving. Keep refrigerated up to one week.

Calories 243 Carbohydrates 3.4g Fat 25g Protein 2.4g

SIDE DISHES

ARTICHOKES IN OLIVE SAUCE

The pungent flavor of garlic and the tangy taste of meaty black olives combine beautifully with artichoke hearts in this Italian side dish.

SERVES 2-4
INGREDIENTS

¼ cup olive oil
1 tablespoon onion, diced
3 garlic cloves, diced
1 teaspoon tapioca flour
1 cup whole milk
½ cup black olives, sliced or minced
1 ½ cups artichoke hearts, thawed
1 teaspoon lemon juice
2 teaspoons Italian seasoning
¼ teaspoon salt
½ teaspoon white pepper

1. In a large skillet, heat the oil on medium heat and cook the onion and garlic until soft.
2. In a medium-size mixing bowl, whisk together the tapioca flour and milk.
3. Add the flour and milk blend to the skillet and continue to stir until thickened.
4. Add the olives, artichokes, lemon, Italian seasoning, salt, and pepper and continue to cook another 3-4 minutes.

COOK'S NOTE

Frozen artichoke hearts are used in this recipe to make it easier to prepare. Steaming and taking apart fresh artichokes to get to the hearts is a lot of work. Canned artichoke hearts tend to be mushy and, because of BPA toxicity shouldn't be used, but the jarred version could be a replacement for frozen. Since the jarred version is usually in brine or marinated, rinse them well before using them in this recipe.

NUTRITIONAL INFORMATION
Calories 260 Carbohydrate 21g Fat 19g Protein 4g

CHEESY ASPARAGUS CAKES

Fresh asparagus teams up with parmesan cheese in these delicious pan fried cakes.

SERVES 6
INGREDIENTS

Salted water, for boiling
2 cups asparagus, cut in 1 inch pieces
¼ teaspoon onion powder
¼ teaspoon dried thyme
1 egg, beaten
½ cup parmesan cheese, shredded
¼ cup rice flour
1 tablespoon butter

1. Bring ½ inch salted water to a boil in a large skillet; then add the asparagus.
2. Cook the asparagus for about 7 minutes until asparagus is tender.
3. Drain and transfer to a medium-size mixing bowl.
4. Crush the asparagus pieces and add the onion, thyme, egg, parmesan, and rice flour. Mix well.
5. In a large skillet, heat the butter over medium heat.
6. Drop large spoonfuls of the asparagus mixture into the heated butter. Press each with the back of a spoon to flatten into patties and fry about 2-3 minutes on each side until golden brown.
7. Transfer to a serving dish and continue with the remaining mixture. Makes 10-12 cakes. (You may need to turn the heat down to medium-low and add more butter for the second batch.)

COOK'S NOTE

Asparagus doesn't have to be completely pureed in this recipe. You want to have some texture in each cheesy bite of these fried cakes.

NUTRITIONAL INFORMATION
Calories 112 Carbohydrate 13g Fat 5g Protein 5g

SPICY BOK CHOY IN GARLIC SAUCE

This super simple, fast stir-fry gives bok choy a kick with a spicy and sweet garlic sauce made from combining garlic and ginger with dark molasses.

SERVES 4
INGREDIENTS

1 large bok choy, chopped
1 tablespoon olive oil
1 tablespoon butter or ghee, melted
¼ cup water
¼ teaspoon dried ginger
3 cloves garlic, minced
1 tablespoon dark molasses
1 teaspoon salt
¼ teaspoon white pepper

1. Trim off the ends of the bok choy and chop, keeping the white parts separate from the green as they will need to cook longer. Set aside.
2. In a small bowl stir together the olive oil and the butter or ghee.
3. In a separate larger bowl, stir together the water, ginger, garlic, and molasses. Set this aside.
4. Heat the oil and butter or ghee in a large skillet or wok over medium-high heat.
5. Add the bok choy stems first; stir fry for a few minutes or until the pieces start to turn a pale green. When stems are almost cooked, add the leaves. Cook and stir until leaves are wilted, 1 to 2 minutes.
6. Pour the water, ginger, garlic, and molasses mix into the skillet
7. Cook, stirring constantly, until sauce has thickened slightly, about 2 minutes.
8. Add the salt and pepper and serve.

COOK'S NOTE

Bok choy is a type of Chinese cabbage. You might find it at the market under different names like Chinese white cabbage, pak choi or pok choi. It is green and leafy at the top and looks a little like romaine. It has a round white bulb on the bottom and slightly resembles celery or rhubarb.

NUTRITIONAL INFORMATION
Calories 101 Carbohydrate 9g Fat 6.7g Protein 3g

CARAMELIZED ACORN SQUASH

A simple, sweet, and delicate desert.

SERVES 2
INGREDIENTS

2 acorn squash, cut in half and seeds removed
2 tablespoons butter
2 teaspoons honey
½ teaspoon salt

1. Preheat oven to 425 degrees.
2. Place acorn squash on a baking sheet cut side up.
3. Place 1 tablespoon butter and 1 teaspoon honey in each acorn half.
4. Sprinkle with salt.
5. Bake for 45-50 minutes or until squash is tender and serve.

COOK'S NOTE

Winter squash is in fact a truly delicious way to squeeze in an extra serving of vegetables. You can't go wrong with this sweet, buttery, dessert-like vegetable.

NUTRITIONAL INFORMATION
Calories 127 Carbohydrate 25g Fat 4g Protein 2g

SAUTÉED ASPARAGUS

Tender asparagus stalks cooked in olive oil, garlic and herbs.

SERVES 4
INGREDIENTS

3 tablespoons olive oil
2 garlic cloves, minced
1 bunch asparagus, ends trimmed
1 teaspoon onion powder
¼ teaspoon salt
¼ teaspoon white pepper
1 teaspoon dried oregano
1 tablespoon white wine vinegar
1 tablespoon water

1. In a skillet, heat the oil and the garlic over high heat.
2. Add the trimmed asparagus, onion powder, salt, pepper, and oregano. Cook for 4 minutes.
3. Reduce heat to medium. Then add the white wine vinegar and water. Cover and cook another 4 minutes or until the ends are easily pierced.

COOK'S NOTE
Cooking time for asparagus depends on the size of the spears. If the spears are thick, increase the cooking time to 5 or 6 minutes.

NUTRITIONAL INFORMATION
Calories 116 Carbohydrate 5g Fat 10.3g Protein 2g

SLOW COOKER BUTTERNUT SQUASH
Using a slow cooker to makes it easy to prepare this simple, delicious, rich, and healthy side dish.

SERVES 4
INGREDIENTS

1 large butternut squash.
2 tablespoons butter

1. Place the whole squash in a large slow cooker and heat on low for 5-6 hours or on high for 3-4 hours.
2. Turn off the cooker and allow the squash to cool before removing and cutting it in half.
3. Scoop the cooked squash out of the shell and add the butter. Stir and serve.

COOK'S NOTE
A cup of butternut squash provides 582 mg of potassium, more than the amount available in a banana.

NUTRITIONAL INFORMATION
Calories 87 Carbohydrate 13g Fat 4g Protein 1g

BOK CHOY STIR-FRY

Tender chopped bok choy and a touch of molasses give this quick Chinese stir-fry a mildly sweet flavor.

SERVES 4
INGREDIENTS

2 tablespoons coconut oil or ghee
½ medium onion, sliced thin
½ red or yellow bell pepper, sliced thin
2 garlic cloves, chopped
1 head bok choy, trimmed and chopped
½ teaspoon dark molasses
¼ teaspoon balsamic vinegar
¼ teaspoon dried ginger
¼ teaspoon red pepper flakes
¼ teaspoon salt

1. In a large skillet or wok, heat the oil over medium-high heat.
2. Add the onion, sliced pepper, and garlic.
3. Stir-fry for about 4 minutes until soft.
4. Add in the bok choy, molasses, vinegar, ginger, red pepper flakes, and salt.
5. Cook another 2-3 minutes until greens are wilted and stalks are crisp-tender.
6. Serve hot.

COOK'S NOTE

Bok choy is a type of Chinese cabbage that's very tender and rich in nutrients including omega-3, zinc, vitamin C, and vitamin K. The combination of balsamic vinegar, molasses, ginger and salt is a healthy alternative to soy sauce.

NUTRITIONAL INFORMATION
Calories 100 Carbohydrate 8g Fat 7g Protein 3g

TEX-MEX SPAGHETTI SQUASH

Silky spaghetti squash topped with seasoned corn and melted cheese.

SERVES 6-8
INGREDIENTS

1 spaghetti squash, cooked
1 cup cheddar, shredded and divided
2 tablespoons butter
1 medium onion, chopped
1 cup corn
1 medium tomato, diced
½ teaspoon chili powder
1 teaspoon cumin
¼ teaspoon garlic powder
¼ teaspoon salt
¼ teaspoon white pepper

1. Slice the cooked squash in half and remove the peel and seeds.
2. Line the bottom of a 9x13 casserole dish with the squash and press it down.
3. Top the squash with half of the cheddar cheese.
4. In a large skillet, melt the butter over medium-high heat and cook the onion for about 3 minutes until soft.
5. Add the corn and stir-fry about 2 minutes (if using frozen corn cook an extra minute). Then add the tomato and cook 1 more minute.
6. Pour the cooked onion, corn, and tomato over the squash, spread it out evenly, and season with chili powder, cumin, garlic powder, salt, and pepper.
7. Top with the remaining cheese and place the dish under the broiler for about 2-3 minutes to melt the cheese.
8. Serve hot.

COOK'S NOTE
The simplest way to have cooked squash already prepared for this dinner is to put it in the slow cooker in the morning. Puncture it a few times with a sharp knife and cook it on low for 6-8 hours.

NUTRITIONAL INFORMATION
Calories 212 Carbohydrate 23g Fat 11g Protein 8g

BROCCOLI MASH

A healthy, nutritious dish full of fiber and flavor.

SERVES 4
INGREDIENTS

1 head broccoli, chopped into florets or 16 ounces frozen broccoli florets
1 teaspoon dried basil
4 tablespoons butter
1 teaspoon garlic powder
⅓ cup whole milk yogurt or sour cream
Salt and pepper, as desired

1. Chop the broccoli into florets or use frozen broccoli florets.
2. Boil the broccoli in plenty of water for 7 minutes. Drain and discard the water.
3. Add the basil and blend in a food processor or use an immersion blender. Then add the butter, garlic, yogurt or sour cream, and salt and pepper.
4. Stir until the butter melts and serve.

COOK'S NOTE

This is a great substitute for mashed potatoes. Looks amazing on a plate and is really easy to make.

NUTRITIONAL INFORMATION
Calories 120 Carbohydrate 4g Fat 11.7g Protein 2g

BUFFALO CAULIFLOWER

Fully loaded with the awesome flavor of buffalo chicken wings, these low carb and vegetarian buffalo cauliflower bites have a soft and tender inside and crispy outside.

SERVES 4
INGREDIENTS

2 tablespoons butter
2 tablespoons Tabasco sauce
2 cups fresh cauliflower florets
2 tablespoons olive oil
½ tsp salt
½ teaspoon garlic powder

1. Preheat the oven to 450 degrees.
2. Line a rimmed baking sheet with parchment paper.
3. In a small saucepan, melt the butter and whisk in the Tabasco. Set aside.
4. In a large bowl, toss the cauliflower florets with the olive oil, salt and garlic powder.
5. Spread on the baking sheet and roast until tender-crisp, about 15 minutes.
6. Switch the oven to broil and set an oven rack about 6 inches below the heat element.
7. Add the roasted cauliflower back to the large bowl and mix in the hot sauce mixture.
8. Return the cauliflower florets to the baking sheet and broil until browned and bubbly, keeping a close eye on them so they don't burn. (About 2-3 minutes.)

COOK'S NOTE
Adding a homemade healthy dip to this recipe is as simple as adding a pinch of dill, salt, garlic powder, onion powder, and lemon juice to a cup of plain whole milk yogurt.

NUTRITIONAL INFORMATION
Calories 215 Carbohydrate 7g Fat 20g Protein 4g

BROCCOLI CHEESE BITES

These baked broccoli cheese bites are an easy, healthy, and delicious snack or side dish.

SERVES 12 (2 broccoli bites each)
INGREDIENTS

1 large bunch of broccoli florets
2 eggs, lightly beaten
¼ cup onion, grated
½ cup, parmesan cheese, grated
¼ cup plain whole milk yogurt or sour cream
1 cup cheddar cheese, grated
1 teaspoon lemon juice
½ teaspoon salt

1. Preheat oven to 350 degrees.
2. Lightly oil 2 mini muffin pans or use paper muffin cups. If using regular muffin tins, simply use less mix in each cup.
3. Chop the broccoli into bite size pieces. In a large saucepan, cover the broccoli with water and bring to a boil. Turn down the heat and simmer for about 3 minutes.
4. Drain and rinse with cold water to stop the cooking. This also reduces the oxalate content.
5. In a large bowl, mix the remaining ingredients and stir in the broccoli.
6. Divide the broccoli mix into the muffin cups and bake for 25 minutes until cooked through and lightly browned on the top.

COOK'S NOTE

With so many delicious flavors and nutrients, you may want to freeze some extras to serve later for a healthy breakfast or snack. Simply prepare the muffins as directed and let them cool before storing in an airtight container. These bites can be kept in the fridge for 3 days or frozen up to 3 months. You can also cook the bites freeform. Just grease a baking sheet or use parchment paper and spoon large dollops of the mixture onto the pan. Baking time is the same.

NUTRITIONAL INFORMATION
Calories 82 Carbohydrate 2g Fat 5.6g Protein 6g

BUTTER BAKED CAULIFLOWER

Butter-roasting infuses cauliflower with a nutty flavor that melts in your mouth.

SERVES 4
INGREDIENTS

1 head cauliflower, cut into bite-sized florets
½ teaspoon salt
¼ teaspoon white pepper
¼ cup butter

1. Preheat the oven to 400 degrees.
2. Cut the cauliflower into small florets; the smaller they are the quicker they will be done.
3. Place in a large baking dish and season with salt and pepper.
4. Sprinkle with melted butter.
5. Bake on the upper rack in the oven for about 20 minutes or more, depending on the size of the florets.

COOK'S NOTE

Cauliflower is rich in antioxidants and anti-inflammatory compounds, which lower oxidative stress and the presence of free radicals in our body.

NUTRITIONAL INFORMATION
Calories 325 Carbohydrate 7g Fat 31g Protein 5g

BALSAMIC SAVOY CABBAGE

An easy to make, quick, healthy fried cabbage with balsamic vinegar.

SERVES 4
INGREDIENTS

2 tablespoons olive oil
1 red onion, chopped
3 garlic cloves, minced
1 savoy cabbage head, chopped
2 teaspoons balsamic vinegar
¼ teaspoon salt
¼ teaspoon white pepper
2 teaspoons white wine vinegar

1. Heat the oil in a large skillet and cook the onion and garlic over medium heat for about 3 minutes.
2. Add the remaining ingredients and cook until the cabbage is tender. (About 6 minutes)

COOK'S NOTE

The leaves of the Savoy cabbage are rather ruffled and have a wonderful green color on the outside, turning to light green and then yellow on the inside. Its flavor is mild, and it cooks much quicker compared to other cabbages. It contains important antioxidants like sulforaphane and kaempferol that help keep inflammation in check.

NUTRITIONAL INFORMATION
calories 101 Carbohydrate 9g Fat 6.9 Protein 2g

CURRIED CAULIFLOWER

The Indian spices and tomato combination adds an exotic flavor and color to cauliflower.

SERVES 4
INGREDIENTS

1 onion, diced
2 garlic cloves, minced
1 tomato, chopped
1 teaspoon dried basil
1 ½ teaspoons curry powder
½ teaspoon dried ginger or 1 ½ tablespoon fresh minced ginger
½ teaspoon red pepper flakes
1 tablespoon butter
1 cup water
½ medium head cauliflower florets, cut bite size

1. In a medium-size saucepan, bring the onion, garlic, tomato, basil, curry powder, ginger, red pepper flakes, butter and water to a boil.
2. Reduce heat to medium, add the cauliflower florets, and continue to simmer for about 12 minutes. Stir occasionally and check for tenderness.
3. Serve hot.

COOK'S NOTE

A perfect, spicy side dish for fish or chicken but can also be served as a vegetarian main dish when served with rice or lentils.

NUTRITIONAL INFORMATION
Calories 62 Carbohydrate 8g Fat 3 g Protein 2g

BUTTERED CABBAGE

A pure and simple side dish loaded with a sweet buttery flavor.

SERVES 4
INGREDIENTS

½ large green or purple head of cabbage
½ cup butter
¼ teaspoon salt
⅛ teaspoon pepper

1. Remove outer leaves, cut in half, and remove the core of the cabbage.
2. Halve the sections again and slice the cabbage into thin shreds.
3. In a large skillet, melt the butter over medium-heat, and then add the cabbage, salt, and pepper.
4. Cook for about 5 minutes, stirring occasionally, and then cover.
5. Turn the heat down to medium-low and continue to cook for about 5 minutes more or until the cabbage is tender.
6. Serve hot.

COOK'S NOTE

A great accompaniment to pork, beef, or chicken. One serving of this buttery cabbage supplies 100% of your vitamin K requirements.

NUTRITIONAL INFORMATION
Calories 232 Carbohydrate 7g Fat 23g Protein 2g

VEGETABLE FRIED RICE

Each bite of this simple stir-fried rice offers a colorful mix of flavors.

SERVES 4-6
INGREDIENTS

2 tablespoons coconut oil or ghee
1 red onion, chopped
3 garlic cloves, minced
¼ cup carrot, chopped
¼ cup yellow or red bell pepper, chopped
½ cup cabbage, chopped, (any type cabbage works well)
½ cup green peas, (frozen is fine)

1 tablespoon water
1 teaspoon balsamic vinegar
1 teaspoon dark molasses
¼ teaspoon ginger
2 eggs, beaten
2 cups cooked rice
½ teaspoon salt
¼ teaspoon pepper

1. In a large skillet or wok, heat the oil over high heat.
2. Add the onion, garlic, carrot, and bell pepper and stir fry for about 3 minutes until soft.
3. Stir in the cabbage, peas, water, vinegar, molasses, and ginger. Cook for 3 minutes, stirring constantly.
4. Add the beaten eggs and continue to stir-fry until the eggs are cooked.
5. Add the cooked rice and stir-fry until mixed thoroughly with the vegetables.
6. Season with salt and pepper and serve hot.

COOK'S NOTE
If you desire a less sticky rice cook the rice ahead of time and refrigerate. Additional time will be needed to stir-fry until the dish is hot. The traditional soy sauce or tamari are not needed to enjoy fried rice dishes. Both are made from soybeans which are high in oxalates and unless bought organic are often genetically modified. A healthy alternative to soy sauce is the combination of balsamic vinegar, molasses, ginger and salt.

NUTRITIONAL INFORMATION
Calories 311 Carbohydrate 49g Fat 9g Protein 8g

CARIBBEAN SLAW

A mayonnaise free slaw that's light and fruity. It's the perfect no-cook side dish for fish or chicken.

SERVES 4
INGREDIENTS

2 tablespoons Dijon mustard
1 tablespoon honey
2 tablespoons white wine vinegar or lemon juice
1 teaspoon garlic, minced
1 teaspoon Tabasco sauce
2 tablespoons olive oil
3 tablespoons apricot jam
2 tablespoons plain whole milk yogurt
Salt and pepper as desired
1 head savoy cabbage, shredded

1. Add all of the first 9 ingredients to a large mixing bowl and whisk together until fully combined.
2. Add in the cabbage and toss well to combine.
3. Refrigerate for at least 20 minutes before serving.

COOK'S NOTE

Cabbage contains many different antioxidants that have been shown to reduce chronic inflammation. In fact, research has shown that eating more cruciferous vegetables reduces certain blood markers of inflammation.

NUTRITIONAL INFORMATION
Calories 157 Carbohydrate 23g Fat 7.5g Protein 3g

GREEK SLAW

This delicious Greek slaw recipe is mayo-free yet creamy, light, quick and easy to prepare.

SERVES 4
INGREDIENTS

4 cups cabbage, shredded
½ cup shredded carrots
½ cup green onions, chopped
⅔ cup plain whole milk yogurt
1 teaspoon lemon juice
2 tablespoons white wine vinegar
2 tablespoons honey
1 teaspoon Dijon mustard
⅛ teaspoon salt
⅛ teaspoon white pepper

1. Combine the cabbage, carrots and green onions in a large bowl and toss.
2. In a separate bowl, whisk together yogurt, lemon juice, vinegar, honey, mustard, salt, and pepper until combined.
3. Pour the yogurt mixture into the cabbage mixture and toss until evenly combined.
4. Serve immediately or cover and refrigerate for up to 4 hours.

COOK'S NOTE

Use plain full fat yogurt. Do not try 0% or 2% yogurt, recipe won't work. Any vinegar except balsamic will work – white, white wine, red wine, or apple cider vinegar.

NUTRITIONAL INFORMATION
Calories 95 Carbohydrate 19g Fat 1.6g Protein 3g

CREAMED BOK CHOY
Loads of flavor for a quick and simple side dish.

SERVES 2
INGREDIENTS

2 tablespoons olive oil
2 tbsp butter
2 cloves garlic, minced
1 cup heavy whipping cream
1 tablespoon maple syrup
4 cups bok choy, chopped
salt and pepper, to taste

1. Heat butter and olive oil in a frying pan over medium-high heat.
2. Add garlic and cook for 1 minute.
3. Add cream and maple syrup and bring to a light boil. Simmer for 4-5 minutes in order for the sauce to reduce by a third.
4. Add in the bok choy and bring to a boil for another minute. The sauce should coat the bok choy completely.
5. Season with salt and pepper and serve immediately.

COOK'S NOTE
Bok choy, also called Chinese cabbage is a member of the Brassica cabbage family. Bok choy is highly nutritious, high in calcium, and very low in carbs.

NUTRITIONAL INFORMATION
Calories 478 Carbohydrate 12.5g Fat 48g Protein 3.7g

BLACK-EYED PEA CAKES
These savory cakes are the perfect Southern-inspired appetizer or side dish.

SERVES 2
INGREDIENTS

2-3 tablespoons olive oil for frying
1 garlic clove minced
½ small onion, diced
½ teaspoon cumin
½ teaspoon white pepper

2 cups cooked black-eyed peas
1 egg
1 tablespoon olive oil
¼ cup corn flour
¼ teaspoon cilantro
¼ teaspoon salt
¼ teaspoon white pepper

1. In a medium-size skillet, heat 2 tablespoons of olive oil. Add the garlic and onion and garlic and cook over moderate heat just until softened, about 3 minutes.
2. Add the cumin and white pepper and cook until fragrant, about 1 minute. Scrape the onion mixture into the bowl of a food processor. Add 1 cups of the black-eyed peas and pulse until the mixture is finely chopped but not smooth.
3. Scrape the mixture into a medium bowl. Mix in the remaining whole black-eyed peas, egg, olive oil, corn flour and seasonings.
4. Form the mixture into twelve ¼ cup patties, about ½ inch thick.
5. In a very large skillet, heat 1/8 inch of oil until simmering. Add the cakes and fry over medium heat until golden brown, about 2 minutes per side.
6. Drain on paper towels. Serve the black-eyed pea cakes as a side dish.

COOK'S NOTE
Black-eyed peas are a huge part of the rich food culture of the South and have been in Southern recipes for generations. If you're looking for a veggie burger recipe that doesn't involve black beans, make the patties a little bit larger and purée more of the black-eyed peas.
Optional toppings include, sour cream, avocado or simply garnish with cilantro.

NUTRITIONAL INFORMATION
Calories 335 Carbohydrate 45.8g Fat 11.9g Protein 16.1g

COCONUT RICE

Coconut milk lends fat and sweetness to rice, making it a rich mellow side dish.

SERVES 2
INGREDIENTS

1 cup coconut milk
1 cup water
1 cup uncooked rice
1 pinch salt

1. In a medium sized pot, add the coconut milk, water, rice and salt.
2. On high heat, allow the mixture to boil. Once it starts to boil, turn the heat down to low and cook covered for 20 minutes.
3. Fluff and serve.

COOK'S NOTE

Coconut rice is a rich, savory side dish that goes well with Asian and Asian-inspired dishes. This rice is a savory coconut rice, not the sweet dessert coconut rice.

NUTRITIONAL INFORMATION
Calories 261 Carbohydrate 35g Fat 16.3g Protein 12g

GARLIC ROASTED VEGETABLES

Oven roasted vegetables are quick, easy to prepare, and packed full of nutrition and flavor.

SERVES 4
INGREDIENTS

1 cup broccoli florets
2 cups zucchini, chopped
2 yellow squash, chopped
1 red bell pepper, chopped
1 red onion, chopped
2 tablespoons olive oil
4 cloves garlic, minced
1 teaspoon dried oregano

Salt and pepper, as desired

1. Preheat oven to 425 degrees.
2. Lightly oil a parchment lined baking sheet.
3. Add all of the cut vegetables, the oil, garlic, and oregano to a large bowl and toss to coat.
4. Spread the vegetables out on the baking sheet in a single layer.
5. Sprinkle with salt and pepper as desired.
6. Bake for 12-15 minutes, or until tender, and serve immediately.

COOK'S NOTE
Baking time may need to be adjusted depending on the thickness of the vegetables.

NUTRITIONAL INFORMATION
Calories 104 Carbohydrate 10g Fat 7.1g Protein 3g

BASIL PESTO RICE
A healthy side dish that features the bold flavors of fresh basil, garlic, and parmesan cheese making it the perfect pairing to chicken.

SERVES 2
INGREDIENTS

1 cup Basmati or long-grain white rice
2 cups chicken broth or water
3 tablespoons olive oil
2 cloves garlic, minced
1 cup fresh basil
¼ cup parmesan cheese, grated
Salt and pepper, to taste

1. In a medium saucepan, combine rice, broth, olive oil and garlic.
2. Bring to a boil. Reduce heat. Cover and cook on low for 20 minutes, or until all of the liquid has been absorbed.
3. Remove rice from heat and stir in the basil and parmesan cheese.
4. Season with salt and pepper, to taste. Serve immediately.

COOK'S NOTE
This basil pesto rice is great with fish or chicken.

NUTRITIONAL INFORMATION
Calories 664 Carbohydrate 81g Fat 27.1g Protein 22g

OVEN ROASTED CABBAGE STEAKS
This crispy, delicious side dish roasts fresh cabbage with garlic elevating this healthy vegetable to a new level.

SERVES 4
INGREDIENTS

1 head green cabbage, dark loose leaves removed
1 teaspoon garlic powder
2 tablespoons olive oil.
Salt and pepper, as desired

1. Preheat oven to 400 degrees.
2. Slice the cabbage into ½ inch thick steaks
3. Brush with oil on both sides and place onto parchment lined baking sheet.
4. Roast for 17-20 minutes or until caramelized.
5. Salt and pepper as desired. Remove and serve.

COOK'S NOTE
Cook time may have to be adjusted depending on the thickness of the steaks. Cook until tender and brown.

NUTRITIONAL INFORMATION
Calories 111 Carbohydrate 12g Fat 7g Protein 2g

EGG FRIED RICE

A healthy egg fried rice flavored with onions, garlic, and bell peppers.

SERVES 2
INGREDIENTS

2 tablespoons coconut oil or ghee
½ red onion, diced
½ red bell pepper, diced
2 garlic cloves, minced
4 eggs, beaten
1 cup rice, cooked
¼ teaspoon salt
⅛ teaspoon white pepper

1. In a nonstick skillet, heat the oil or ghee over high heat.
2. Add the onion, bell pepper and garlic. Stir fry for about 3 minutes or until soft.
3. Lower the heat to medium and add the beaten eggs. Continue to stir fry until the eggs are cooked.
4. Add the cooked rice and continue to stir fry until mixed thoroughly.
5. Season with salt and pepper and serve hot.

COOK'S NOTE

Fried rice is usually a dish that you make to repurpose the leftover cooked rice from the day before. You want to avoid freshly cooked rice because it is still moist and steamy, which may yield fried rice with a creamier texture.

NUTRITIONAL INFORMATION
Calories 615 Carbohydrate 83g Fat 22.6g Protein 18g

MASHED LIMA BEANS

Lima beans whipped into a mashed-potato style texture that is creamy and full of flavor.

SERVES 4
INGREDIENTS

2 cups water
1 teaspoon salt
2 garlic cloves, minced
1 teaspoon dried rosemary
16 oz frozen baby lima beans
1 tablespoon olive oil

1. Bring water, salt, garlic, and rosemary to a boil in a large pot.
2. Add lima beans and cook for 18 minutes, or until very soft.
3. Drain, reserving ½ cup of the cooking liquid.
4. Pour into a blender and process until smooth, adding the olive oil and the reserved liquid a small amount at a time until you reach the consistency of mashed potatoes.
5. Add the mashed beans to a bowl and serve.

COOK'S NOTE
Serve warm as a side dish or cover and cool in the refrigerator to use a dip.

NUTRITIONAL INFORMATION
Calories 182 Carbohydrate 29g Fat 3.9g Protein 9g

POTATO EGG NEST

Tender-but-crispy potato nests with a luscious baked egg in the middle.

SERVES 6
INGREDIENTS

3 medium red potatoes
Salt and pepper, to taste
12 whole large eggs

1. Preheat the oven to 400 degrees.
2. Bake the potatoes until almost tender (potatoes should still have a little bite) 45 minutes to 1 hour.
3. Allow to cool, remove the peel, and grate them in a large bowl. Season with salt and pepper.
4. Increase oven temperature to 425 degrees.
5. Oil a 12-cup muffin pan. Scoop 3-4 tablespoons of potato into each muffin cup and gently press the sides and bottom in each muffin cup to make a nest. Don't press the potatoes firmly against the pan; they should sit lightly in the pan.
6. Bake for 15 to 20 minutes. Watch and make sure they do not burn.
7. Remove from the oven when the nests are golden brown and allow them to cool.
8. Crack an egg into each nest and bake until the whites are set, about 15 minutes.
9. Remove from muffin pan with a spoon or fork and serve.

COOK'S NOTE
Eggs offer satisfying protein, essential amino acids, heart-healthy fats, vitamin D (which is difficult to find through food), B vitamins, vitamin A, and potassium.

NUTRITIONAL INFORMATION
Calories 221 Carbohydrate 18g Fat 9.7g Protein 15g

STUFFED ZUCCHINI
Light, healthy yet tasty zucchinis loaded with Italian flavor.

SERVES 2
INGREDIENTS

2 medium zucchini squashes
2 tablespoons olive oil
½ cup red onion, diced
2 garlic cloves minced
½ cup red bell pepper, diced
1 teaspoon dried oregano
1 teaspoon dried basil
½ teaspoon salt
¼ teaspoon white pepper
¼ cup parmesan cheese, grated or shredded
¼ cup cheddar, shredded
Additional grated parmesan to sprinkle over cooked squash

1. Preheat oven to 375 degrees.
2. Trim stem ends from squash. Cut about 1/3 off the top of each squash horizontally. Then cut a small horizontal sliver from the bottom so that the squash will sit flat and not roll.
3. Dice the cut off tops and set aside.
4. Scoop out some of the inside of the squash making it look like a canoe.
5. In a large skillet or frying pan heat the oil over medium heat and add the onion and garlic. Cook about 2 minutes.
6. Add the red bell pepper and cut up zucchini tops as well as the scooped-out zucchini. Mix and cook about 1 minute more.
7. Remove from heat and mix in oregano, basil, salt, pepper, and both cheeses.
8. Divide the filling between each zucchini boat and press into the squash.
9. Bake for 30–35 minutes uncovered. As soon as they come out of the oven, sprinkle the tops with additional parmesan cheese and serve.

COOK'S NOTE
Zucchini squash is low in carbohydrates and calories, and are brimming with fiber and vitamin C, which helps promote a healthy immune system.

NUTRITIONAL INFORMATION
Calories 148 Carbohydrate 7g Fat 11.7g Protein 5g

SLOW COOKER RATATOUILLE
A combination of fresh summer produce, slow cooked to a rich flavorful stew.

SERVES 4
INGREDIENTS

3 tomatoes, quartered
2 zucchinis, sliced thick
2 yellow squash, sliced thick
1 cup cauliflower florets
1 red or yellow bell pepper, chopped
1 medium onion, chopped
½ cup black olives, halved or sliced
4 tablespoons olive oil
4 garlic cloves, diced
1 teaspoon fresh dried basil
½ teaspoon dried thyme
¼ teaspoon salt
⅛ teaspoon pepper
½ cup parmesan cheese, grated (optional)

1. Combine all of the ingredients except the parmesan cheese in a slow cooker and mix well.
2. Cook on low heat for 6-8 hours or on high for 3-4 hours.
3. Serve hot.

COOK'S NOTE
The traditional French ratatouille is usually prepared as a thick stew with each vegetable sautéed individually and then combined and baked. This slow cooker version is equally terrific in taste and much simpler to prepare. Serve it as a side dish to any meat or pour it over rice or eggs and top with cheese for a main dish.

NUTRITIONAL INFORMATION
Calories 227 Carbohydrate 18g Fat 17g Protein 5g

SAUTÉED BRUSSELS SPROUTS

These tiny cabbages simply sautéed with tomato and onion create a flavorful one skillet vegetarian dish or can be paired with fish or chicken.

SERVES 4
INGREDIENTS

1 tablespoon butter
2 cloves garlic, chopped
½ onion, chopped
2 medium tomatoes, chopped
¼ teaspoon salt
½ teaspoon red pepper flakes
½ teaspoon dried thyme
1 teaspoon dried basil
1 ½ cups fresh or frozen Brussels sprouts, thawed and halved
½ cup water
Parmesan cheese (as desired)

1. In a large skillet, heat the butter over medium heat, and then add the garlic and onion. Cook for about 3 minutes until soft.
2. Add the tomatoes, salt, pepper flakes, thyme, and basil. Continue to cook another 2 minutes until tomatoes are tender.
3. Add the halved Brussels sprouts and water and continue to cook over medium heat another 15 minutes with occasional stirring.
4. Serve hot topped with parmesan as desired.

COOK'S NOTE
Brussels sprouts are related to a wild variety of cabbage that originated near the Mediterranean. They are named after the city of Brussels in Belgium. Brussels sprouts are high in protein, low in carbohydrate, and are high in vitamins C, K, and A.

NUTRITIONAL INFORMATION
Calories 78 Carbohydrate 11g Fat 3g Protein 4g

SAVORY SAVOY SLAW

A tender, tangy, and fresh tasting slaw with a hint of creaminess to bind it together.

SERVES 4-6
INGREDIENTS

½ head savoy cabbage
¼ cup white wine vinegar
¼ cup honey
2 tablespoons plain whole milk yogurt or sour cream
2 tablespoons olive oil
½ teaspoon salt
¼ teaspoon white pepper
¼ teaspoon crushed red pepper flakes

1. Slice the cabbage in half through the core. Cut a v-shaped notch around the white core and discard the core. Slice lengthwise into quarters and thinly slice each quarter crosswise into strips.
2. In a medium-size mixing bowl, whisk together the wine vinegar, honey, yogurt, oil, salt, and peppers.
3. Pour the dressing over the shredded cabbage. Mix well.
4. Allow to sit for about 15 minutes, stirring occasionally to meld the flavors during this time.
5. Can be served room temperature or chilled.

COOK'S NOTE

Any cabbage can be used in this recipe. Green is the most common and red cabbage will give the slaw a more peppery flavor. Savoy cabbage has the most delicate flavor and a little less crunch. If green or red cabbage is used, add another ¼ teaspoon salt and let it sit at least 30 minutes before serving.

NUTRITIONAL INFORMATION
Calories 112 Carbohydrate 12g Fat 7g Protein 0g

SLOW COOKER INDIAN LENTILS

A fragrant traditional Indian side dish of protein rich lentils spiced up with curry, cumin, and cayenne.

SERVES 4-6
INGREDIENTS

2 cups green or yellow lentils
2 tablespoons coconut oil, olive oil or ghee
½ teaspoon curry powder
½ teaspoon dry mustard
¼ teaspoon cumin
½ teaspoon cayenne pepper
¼ teaspoon dried ginger
3 cloves garlic, chopped
1 small onion, chopped
2 medium tomatoes, chopped
4 cups chicken or bone broth
Salt (as desired) *

1. Sort and rinse the lentils under warm water.
2. Spread the oil over the bottom of the slow cooker.
3. Add all ingredients to the slow cooker and mix well.
4. Cover and cook on low for 6-8 hours or on high for 3-4 hours.
5. Serve hot.

COOK'S NOTE

Unlike most dried beans or legumes, lentils require no soaking before cooking. Lentils are a good source of magnesium and fiber. These hearty lentils may be served with rice or any meat, poultry, or fish.

*Salt will toughen lentils if added during the cooking time, so it's best to salt them after they are cooked.

NUTRITIONAL INFORMATION
Calories 461 Carbohydrate 64g Fat 9g Protein 31g

SLOW COOKER PEAS AND GREENS

Slow cooked black-eyed peas and greens is a great Southern comfort food that is as healthy as it is delicious.

SERVES 4
INGREDIENTS

2 cups dried black-eyed peas
5 cups water
2 tablespoons olive oil
½ red bell pepper, diced
1 medium onion, diced
3 garlic cloves, minced
1 teaspoon oregano
1 teaspoon white pepper
1 large bok choy, trimmed and chopped
1 teaspoon salt.

1. Sort and rinse the black-eyed peas under warm water.
2. Spread the oil in the bottom of the slow cooker.
3. Place all of the ingredients except the bok choy and the salt in a slow cooker.
4. Cover and cook on low for 6-8 hours or on high for 3-4 hours.
5. Add in the bok choy and salt and allow to cook another 15 minutes before serving.

COOK'S NOTE

If using a frozen package of black-eyed peas this can be made on the stovetop following package directions. Simply eliminate the extra water from the recipe and add the remaining ingredients.

NUTRITIONAL INFORMATION
Calories 507 Carbohydrate 67g Fat 12g Protein 34g

VEGETABLE RISOTTO

A rich and creamy vegetable and rice Italian comfort food that can be served as a side or main dish.

SERVES 2
INGREDIENTS

4 cups water or vegetable broth
2 tablespoons olive oil
½ medium red onion, finely chopped
3 garlic cloves, minced
½ teaspoon salt
1 ½ cup rice
2 medium zucchinis, diced
2 tablespoons butter
½ cup parmesan cheese, plus more for serving

1. In a small saucepan, bring the water to a boil.
2. In a large saucepan, heat the oil, and add the onion, garlic, and salt.
3. Cook until the onion has softened, about 5 minutes.
4. Add the rice to the large saucepan and cook, stirring occasionally, until the kernels start to crackle, about 1 to 2 minutes.
5. Pour a ladleful of water over the rice and let simmer, stirring constantly, until the rice absorbs the water and the bottom of the pot is nearly dry. Continue adding water a little at a time. Stir constantly, until the rice is nearly al dente, about 20 minutes.
6. Add the zucchini and continue to cook until the rice is tender on the outside but still has some resistance when you bite into it, about 5 minutes more.
7. Stir in the butter and parmesan
8. Top with additional parmesan and serve.

COOK'S NOTE
The key to risotto is stirring often in order to lure starch from the grains.

NUTRITIONAL INFORMATION
Calories 440 Carbohydrate 49g Fat 33.4 Protein 14g

VEGETABLE LOADED MACARONI AND CHEESE

A healthy vegetable loaded macaroni and cheese recipe.

SERVES 6
INGREDIENTS

1 pound elbow macaroni
½ cup water
1 cup cauliflower florets
1 cup zucchini, diced
½ cup carrot, sliced
1 cup pureed pumpkin
2 cups milk
2 cups cheddar cheese, shredded
4 ounces cream cheese
1 teaspoon salt

1. Prepare the macaroni al dente according to package directions.
2. Add water, cauliflower, zucchini, and carrots in a pot over medium heat. Cover and cook until vegetables are tender.
3. Pour the cooked vegetables along with the water into a blender and blend until smooth.
4. Return the blended vegetables to the pot and add in the pumpkin, milk, cheddar cheese, cream cheese and salt. Stir until smooth.
5. Add the macaroni, mix thoroughly, cover and cook on low for about 5 minutes, stirring occasionally.

COOK'S NOTE

Vegetables are always a nice addition to any type of macaroni and cheese not only because they provide another element of flavor and texture, but because they pack in plenty of health benefits.

NUTRITIONAL INFORMATION
Calories 422 Carbohydrate 33g Fat 23.8 Protein 20g

TUSCAN ZUCCHINI AND CORN

A simple side dish full of flavor.

SERVES 4
INGREDIENTS

2 tablespoons olive oil
2 cloves garlic, minced
4 small zucchinis, diced
1 cup corn fresh or frozen
¼ teaspoon dried basil
¼ teaspoon dried oregano
¼ teaspoon salt
½ teaspoon lemon juice
4 tablespoons parmesan, grated

1. Heat olive oil in a large skillet over medium high heat. Add garlic to the skillet and cook, stirring frequently for about 1 minute.
2. Add zucchini, corn, basil, and oregano. Cook, stirring occasionally, until zucchini is tender and cooked through, about 3-4 minutes.
3. Season with salt and stir in lemon juice.
4. Top with parmesan and serve.

COOK'S NOTE

Yellow squash can be used for this recipe, but green zucchini adds a splash of color and adds a little more crunch.

NUTRITIONAL INFORMATION
Calories 129 Carbohydrate 12g Fat 7.6g Protein 4g

SOUTHERN FRIED ZUCCHINI

A classic southern side dish of fresh zucchini coated with cornmeal flour and stir-fried in ghee.

SERVES 2
INGREDIENTS

4 tablespoons ghee
2 large zucchini squash, chopped
½ cup cornmeal

1. In a skillet, heat the ghee over high heat.
2. Place the cut zucchini in a colander and moisten then pour into a bowl.
3. Add the cornmeal and toss to coat.
4. Add to the heated skillet and stir-fry until the cornmeal coating is a golden brown.
5. Reduce heat to medium and cook a couple minutes more until the zucchini is tender.
6. Salt and pepper, as desired.
7. Pour into a paper towel lined bowl and serve.

COOK'S NOTE

Yellow squash can also be used. The squash can be sliced thin as well but this would take a bit more time as they would need to be cooked in batches to prevent them sticking together. This original southern recipe called for bacon fat instead of ghee which is an option if you don't mind using it. Keep in mind that bacon is made from pork and goes through a curing process where it is soaked in salt, nitrates and other ingredients.

NUTRITIONAL INFORMATION
Calories 456 Carbohydrate 57g Fat 23.1g Protein 9g

MAIN DISHES

BEEF AND BUTTERNUT SKILLET
A warm and hearty meal that's also a feast for the eyes.

SERVES 4
INGREDIENTS

2 teaspoons coconut oil, olive oil or ghee
1 medium onion, chopped
½ large red or yellow pepper, chopped
1 pound ground grass-fed beef (or turkey, venison, bison)
3 garlic cloves, chopped
½ teaspoon cayenne pepper
½ teaspoon salt
½ teaspoon white pepper
½ large butternut squash, cooked
1 cup cheddar cheese, grated

1. In a large skillet, heat the coconut oil or ghee over high heat. When hot, add the onion and bell pepper. Cook for about 3 minutes or until soft.
2. Add the beef, garlic, cayenne, salt, and pepper, and stir-fry until the meat is browned.
3. Turn the heat down to medium and add spoonfuls of the cooked butternut squash to the skillet.
4. Stir-fry about a minute to mix the ingredients.
5. Turn off the heat and sprinkle the cheese on top.
6. Allow the cheese to melt and serve.

COOK'S NOTE
To have the butternut squash ready for this recipe, place the whole butternut squash in a slow cooker and cook on low for 6 hours or on high for 4 hours. The leftover half of the squash can be used to make a warm creamy dessert by simply adding a pinch of sea salt, some honey and butter. This delicious skillet dinner is high in vitamin C, B6, B12, niacin, and zinc.

NUTRITIONAL INFORMATION
Calories 428 Carbohydrate 16g Fat 28g Protein 32g

CARIBBEAN COD

This is a tweak on the very traditional Jamaican dish called "Ackee and Saltfish".

SERVES 4
INGREDIENTS

3 tablespoons butter
1 small onion, diced
½ red bell pepper, diced
2 garlic cloves, minced
4 wild-caught (fresh or frozen and thawed) cod fish fillets, patted dry
½ teaspoon salt
½ teaspoon dried thyme
4 eggs, beaten
2 medium stalks scallions, chopped
4 tablespoons black olives, sliced

1. In a large skillet, heat 3 tablespoons butter over medium-high heat, and then add the onions, red bell pepper, and garlic. Cook for about 3 minutes until soft.
2. Add the cod fish, salt, and thyme and turn the heat down to medium. Stir fry another 4 minutes breaking up the cod fish into large chunks.
3. Pour in the eggs and continue to stir until the eggs are scrambled.
4. Garnish the dish with scallions and black olives.
5. Serve hot.

COOK'S NOTE

This delicious dish tastes very similar to the ackee and saltfish which is traditionally served for breakfast in Jamaica. Ackee fruit is cultivated in tropical regions and has a taste and texture very much like scrambled eggs. It is very hard to find in the US. Saltfish is simply a process of drying and salting cod for preservation.

NUTRITIONAL INFORMATION
Calories 299 Carbohydrate 5g Fat 19g Protein 27g

COCONUT CRUSTED COD

The mild, delicate flavor of cod is enhanced with this crispy sweet coconut crust.

SERVES 4
INGREDIENTS

6 tablespoons tapioca flour
¼ teaspoon salt
1 egg, beaten
1 tablespoon honey
½ cup unsweetened coconut, shredded
3 tablespoons coconut oil, olive oil, or ghee
4 wild-caught (fresh or frozen and thawed) cod fish fillets, patted dry

1. In a shallow mixing bowl or plate, blend the flour and salt together.
2. In a separate shallow mixing bowl, beat the eggs, add the honey, and mix well.
3. Spread the coconut out on another plate.
4. In a large skillet, heat oil over medium-high heat.
5. Dredge the fish fillets in the flour, then the egg, and then press both sides into the shredded coconut.
6. Cook on one side to a light golden brown for about 3 minutes. Then turn and cook an additional 2-3 minutes. (If the filets are thick you might need to reduce the heat and cook another 2-3 minutes.)
7. Serve hot.

COOK'S NOTE

Excellent served with vegetable fried rice. Each serving provides 29% of your daily requirement for vitamin B6.

NUTRITIONAL INFORMATION
Calories 476 Carbohydrate 31g Fat 30g Protein 24g

CREOLE-STYLE FISH

Spicy classic Creole-style seasonings bring a depth of flavor to simmered tomatoes and whitefish fillets.

SERVES 2
INGREDIENTS

2 tablespoons butter
2 tablespoons onion, chopped fine
2 garlic cloves, minced
2 tablespoons red bell pepper, chopped fine
2 tablespoons celery, chopped fine
2 cups tomato, chopped
¼ teaspoon cayenne pepper
¼ teaspoon red pepper flakes
¼ teaspoon dried thyme
½ teaspoon dried basil
¼ teaspoon salt
2 fish filets (cod, mahi mahi or grouper) fresh, or thawed and patted dry
1 teaspoon fresh lemon juice

1. In a large skillet, heat the butter over medium-high heat, and then add the onion, garlic, bell pepper, and celery. Cook for about 3 minutes until the vegetables are soft.
2. Add the tomatoes, cayenne pepper, pepper flakes, thyme, basil, and salt.
3. Allow it to come to a boil, and then reduce heat to medium and simmer for about 5 minutes. Stir occasionally.
4. Add the fish and lemon juice and continue to simmer another 6-7 minutes until the fish easily flakes.
5. Serve hot.

COOK'S NOTE

Any type of whitefish works with this spicy tomato-based Creole seasoned sauce. Pour it over rice for a delicious traditional southern Louisiana dish. Each serving provides 35% of your daily requirement for vitamin B6.

NUTRITIONAL INFORMATION
Calories 476 Carbohydrate 31g Fat 30g Protein 24g

JERK CHICKEN PASTA

Chicken marinated in homemade jerk seasoning combine with pasta in this Jamaican-Italian fusion cuisine.

SERVES 4
INGREDIENTS

1 cup water
½ cup white wine vinegar
1 small onion, chopped
1 small red or yellow bell pepper, chopped
3 Serrano peppers, chopped (or 1 teaspoon cayenne pepper)
1 tablespoon allspice
1 teaspoon dried ginger
½ teaspoon salt
½ teaspoon white or black pepper
½ teaspoon dried thyme
¼ teaspoon nutmeg
2 large boneless chicken breasts
3 cups Barilla Gluten-Free Penne or Shells (made with corn flour and rice flour), cooked and drained
¼ cup butter
2 garlic cloves, minced
8 ounces cream cheese
¼ teaspoon salt
¼ teaspoon white or black pepper
¼ teaspoon dried oregano
¼ teaspoon dried basil
½ cup water
Parmesan cheese (as desired)

1. In a small bowl, combine the first 11 ingredients and mix well.
2. Place the chicken breasts in a slow cooker and pour the mixture over the chicken.
3. Cook on low for 6-8 hours or on high for 3-4 hours.
4. Cook the pasta following package directions.
5. As the pasta cooks, prepare the garlic cream sauce by heating the butter and garlic in a large nonstick skillet over medium-high heat for about 30 seconds.
6. Add the cheese, salt, pepper, oregano, basil, and water and reduce heat to a simmer, stirring often.
7. Remove the chicken breasts, shred it, and set aside.

8. Pour the chicken jerk juices into the garlic cream sauce and blend them well.
9. Add the chicken and drained pasta to the skillet. Gently stir the dish to combine all ingredients and serve hot with a sprinkle of parmesan cheese on top.

COOK'S NOTE
There are a lot of ingredients and steps to this creamy pasta dish with spicy authentic jerk seasoning, but when it all comes together it's a very impressive meal rich in vitamin C, niacin, and B6.

Variation: Add fresh cooked asparagus to the meal.

NUTRITIONAL INFORMATION
Calories 585 Carbohydrate 37g Fat 33g Protein 34g

BAKED BUFFALO WINGS
Easy gluten-free restaurant-style buffalo wings that are baked instead of fried.

SERVES 2
INGREDIENTS

8-10 chicken wings
½ cup melted butter
5 ounces Tabasco

1. Preheat oven to 425 degrees.
2. Spread wings out on a parchment lined baking sheet.
3. Bake for 25-30 minutes, turning once.
4. In a large skillet melt the butter, add the Tabasco, then add the cooked wings and toss until the wings are coated.
5. Serve alone or add your own favorite dipping sauce.

COOK'S NOTE
Cook your own buffalo chicken wings instead of using packaged wings which tend to have unhealthy ingredients.

NUTRITIONAL INFORMATION
Calories 580 Carbohydrate 1g Fat 52.2g Protein 30g

KENTUCKY-STYLE BOURBON CHICKEN

Sophisticated yet simple slow cooker bourbon chicken thighs are a traditional southern favorite.

SERVES 4-6
INGREDIENTS

2 tablespoons butter
4-6 chicken thighs
1 tablespoon onion powder
¼ teaspoon garlic powder
¼ cup white wine vinegar
1 tablespoon molasses
¼ cup honey
¼ cup bourbon
¼ cup maple syrup
½ teaspoon dried ginger
¼ teaspoon salt
¼ teaspoon white pepper
1 teaspoon red pepper flakes

1. Spread the butter around the bottom of the slow cooker.
2. Add the chicken.
3. Mix remaining ingredients in a bowl and pour over the chicken.
4. Cook on low for 6-8 hours or on high for 3-4 hours.
5. Serve hot.

COOK'S NOTE

Alcohol burns off during the cooking process and imparts a rich, robust flavor to the chicken thighs.

Variation: 2-3 chicken breasts can be substituted for the thighs.

NUTRITIONAL INFORMATION
Calories 291 Carbohydrate 21g Fat 15g Protein 11g

MEDITERRANEAN SKILLET FRITTATA

A variety of sautéed vegetables, eggs, and cheese create a one skillet meal with rich Italian flavor.

SERVES 4
INGREDIENTS

1 tablespoon butter
⅓ cup red onion, diced
½ cup red or yellow bell pepper, diced
2 cloves garlic, minced
¼ cup button mushrooms, sliced
½ cup tomatoes, diced
½ cup zucchini, diced
1 teaspoon dried Italian spice blend
¼ teaspoon salt
½ teaspoon crushed red pepper flakes
2 tbsp water
4 large eggs, beaten
½ cup black olives, sliced
½ cup parmesan cheese

1. In a large skillet, melt the butter over medium-high heat, and sauté the onions, peppers, garlic, and mushrooms until soft. (About 3 minutes.)
2. Stir in the tomatoes, zucchini, Italian seasoning, salt, red pepper flakes, and water. Cook another 3-4 minutes, stirring often.
3. In a medium-size bowl, beat the eggs and pour evenly across the top of the ingredients in the skillet.
4. Reduce the heat to medium-low and simmer for about 4-5 minutes without stirring.
5. At the end of the cooking time, lightly scrape the top to move any uncooked egg towards the sides of the skillet.
6. Top with olives and parmesan cheese and cook another minute to melt the cheese.
7. Remove from heat, slice like a pizza, and serve hot.

COOK'S NOTE
This quick and filling one skillet protein-packed meal is ideal for breakfast, lunch, or dinner.

NUTRITIONAL INFORMATION
Calories 276 Carbohydrate 9g Fat 19g Protein 18g

PIZZA CASSEROLE

This recipe is more like a deep-dish pizza with an amazing flourless crust.

SERVES 4-6
INGREDIENTS

CRUST
4 ounces cream cheese, softened
2 eggs
¼ teaspoon Italian seasoning
¼ teaspoon garlic powder
¼ cup parmesan cheese (1 ounce)
8 ounces mozzarella cheese, shredded

TOPPINGS
1 red onion, diced
2 cups tomatoes, diced
1 pound grass-fed beef, ground
4 ounces mozzarella cheese, shredded
Optional: Add any of your favorite toppings.

1. Preheat oven to 400 degrees.
2. In a medium-size bowl, blend the softened cream cheese with the eggs, Italian seasonings, and garlic until smooth and creamy.
3. Stir in the parmesan and mozzarella until it's all moistened.
4. Spread the crust mixture evenly in a well-oiled, 9x13 inch glass or ceramic baking dish.
5. Bake 20-25 minutes until evenly browned.
6. Stir-fry the diced onion, tomatoes, and ground beef.
7. Top the crust with cooked onion, tomatoes, ground beef and any optional toppings. Top with mozzarella cheese.
8. Bake at 400 degrees for about 5 minutes or until the cheese is melted.
9. Let stand a few minutes before cutting and serving.

COOK'S NOTE
One serving of this deep-dish pizza supplies 78% of your daily requirement for Vitamin B12 and 43% of your daily requirement for Vitamin B6

NUTRITIONAL INFORMATION
Calories 831 Carbohydrate 33g Fat 54g Protein 54g

PUMPKIN CHILI

This rich, thick, and savory offbeat chili is packed with nutrition as well as flavor.

SERVES 4-6
INGREDIENTS

1 tablespoon coconut oil, olive oil or ghee
1 onion, chopped
1 small red or yellow bell pepper, chopped
3 garlic cloves, minced
1 pound ground grass-fed beef (or turkey, venison, bison)
3 cups tomatoes, diced
1 teaspoon ground cumin
1 teaspoon chili powder
½ teaspoon cayenne pepper
1 teaspoon dried basil
1 ½ cups (12 ounce frozen package) black-eyed peas, purple hull peas or crowder peas.
2 cups water
2 cups pumpkin puree
Salt & pepper (as desired after cooking)

1. In a large pot, heat the coconut oil, olive oil or ghee over medium-high heat, and cook the onion, bell pepper, and garlic. Cook for about 3 minutes, until soft.
2. Add the beef and break it up as it cooks. Cook until the meat is no longer pink.
3. Add diced tomatoes, cumin, chili powder, cayenne, basil, peas, water, and pumpkin to the beef mixture.
4. Bring to a boil and then reduce heat to medium-low. Cover and simmer 35 minutes. Sustain a rolling simmer and stir occasionally.
5. Serve in soup bowls with desired toppings.

COOK'S NOTE
No need to thaw the peas first. Add salt to recipe after it's cooked to avoid tough peas. Black-eyed peas are very low in oxalates making them the perfect "bean" for many recipes. They are especially high in potassium and zinc, which is important for the proper function of all cells.

NUTRITIONAL INFORMATION
Calories 581 Carbohydrate 65g Fat 19g   Protein 41g

SLOW COOKER MUSTARD BARBECUE CHICKEN

This South Carolina style barbecue sauce adds a tangy sweet and spicy flavor to slow cooked chicken breasts.

SERVES 4
INGREDIENTS

1 tablespoon coconut oil, olive oil or ghee
2 boneless chicken breasts
¼ cup white wine vinegar
¼ cup maple syrup
¼ cup water
1 tablespoon molasses
½ cup yellow mustard
3 garlic cloves, crushed
¼ teaspoon paprika
¼ teaspoon cayenne pepper
½ teaspoon onion powder
¼ teaspoon sea salt

1. Spread the oil in the bottom of the slow cooker and add the chicken breasts.
2. In a bowl, mix remaining ingredients and pour over the chicken.
3. Cook on low 6-8 hours or on high for 4 hours.
4. Using two forks, shred the chicken and mix it with the sauce.
5. Serve over rice, on a bun, or with your favorite side dish.

COOK'S NOTE

This simple sauce is so delicious you will never be tempted to buy bottled barbecue sauce again.

NUTRITIONAL INFORMATION
Calories 213 Carbohydrate 10g Fat 6g Protein 29g

SOUTHWEST SALMON CAKES

The rich velvety texture of avocado combined with wild-caught Alaskan salmon and cumin gives these patties a slight southwest flair.

SERVES 4-6
INGREDIENTS

½ avocado
1 egg
¼ teaspoon white pepper
¼ teaspoon dried dill
¼ teaspoon cumin
2 tablespoons onion, diced
2 tablespoons red or yellow bell pepper, diced
1 can (14 ounces) wild-caught Alaskan salmon, well drained
2-3 tablespoons coconut oil or ghee (for frying)
3 roma tomatoes, diced
1 cup corn
2 teaspoons olive oil
3 tablespoons plain whole milk yogurt or sour cream
¼ teaspoon dried basil
¼ teaspoon garlic powder
Salt and pepper (as desired)

1. In a medium-size mixing bowl, mash the avocado and then blend it with the egg, pepper, dill, cumin, onion, and red bell pepper.
2. Stir in the salmon and mix well.
3. In a large skillet, heat the oil over medium-high heat.
4. Form golf ball size balls then flatten a little after placing them in the heated oil. (Makes 8-10 patties.)
5. Cook patties until browned on one side, for about 4-5 minutes, then carefully turn and brown on the other side.
6. In a separate bowl, prepare the topping by combining the tomatoes, corn, oil, yogurt, basil, and garlic. Salt and pepper as desired.
7. Top the salmon cakes with a portion of the topping and serve.

COOK'S NOTE

Two top superfoods are teamed up in these incredibly tasty patties. One serving provides 100% of your daily requirement for vitamin D.

NUTRITIONAL INFORMATION
Calories 394 Carbohydrate 17g Fat 26g Protein 27g

BAKED LEMON ROSEMARY CHICKEN

Lemon and rosemary complement the richly roasted flavor of the chicken in this easy all-in-one dinner.

SERVES 4
INGREDIENTS

1 pound skinless, boneless, chicken breasts, cut 2 x 2 inch squares
2 small red potatoes, quartered
1 red pepper, sliced thick
1 large zucchini or yellow squash, sliced thick
1 large yellow or red onion, cut in 1 inch chunks
¼ cup olive oil
Juice of 1 large lemon
3 cloves fresh garlic, diced
½ teaspoon salt
½ teaspoon dried Italian spices
½ teaspoon dried rosemary

1. Preheat oven to 425 degrees.
2. In a large 16 inch roasting pan, combine all of the ingredients and toss until all ingredients are well coated.
3. Bake 25-30 minutes. Turn on the broiler for the last 2-3 minutes to slightly brown the top. Serve hot.

COOK'S NOTE

Rosemary is a fragrant herb with needle-like leaves that's known for having a wide array of health benefits. You have a winning immune boosting combination when you pair it with garlic and onions in a recipe.

NUTRITIONAL INFORMATION
Calories 225 Carbohydrate 19g Fat 14g Protein 7g

CHICKEN LENTILS

Let your slow cooker do all of the work in this fragrant Indian dish seasoned with curry powder, ginger, and garlic.

SERVES 2
INGREDIENTS

1 cup green or yellow lentils
½ teaspoon curry powder
¼ teaspoon cumin
¼ teaspoon dry mustard
¼ teaspoon dried cilantro
¼ teaspoon white pepper
½ teaspoon cayenne pepper
¼ teaspoon dried ginger
2 cloves garlic, minced
1 small red onion, chopped
1 medium tomato, chopped
3 cups chicken broth or bone broth (can also use water)
2 boneless chicken breasts
Romaine or green leaf lettuce
1 small tomato, diced (optional)

1. Sort and rinse the lentils under warm water.
2. Place the first 12 ingredients in the bottom of a slow cooker and stir a little to mix the spices with the lentils.
3. Place the chicken breasts on top.
4. Cover and cook on low for 6-8 hours or on high for 3-4 hours.
5. Uncover and pull the chicken apart using 2 forks, mixing the chicken into the lentils.
6. Serve in individual bowls with side salad or over romaine leaves and top with a small amount of diced tomato. (optional)

COOK'S NOTE
Unlike most dried beans or legumes, lentils require no soaking before cooking. It's best to salt them after they are cooked because salt will toughen lentils if added during the cooking time. Lentils are a good source of magnesium and fiber.

NUTRITIONAL INFORMATION
Calories 627 Carbohydrate 64g Fat 4g Protein 80g

CHICKEN GUMBO WITH EFFORTLESS ROUX

No need to be in the kitchen all day preparing this Cajun gumbo. The flavorful roux develops simply by frying the chicken in oil.

SERVES 4
INGREDIENTS

¼ cup flour
¼ teaspoon salt
½ teaspoon garlic powder
¼ teaspoon white pepper
¼ teaspoon cayenne pepper
1 pound boneless chicken breasts or thighs, cut in 1 inch pieces
4 tablespoons coconut oil, olive oil or ghee
1 medium red onion, chopped
5 medium tomatoes, chopped
1 teaspoon dried basil
1 teaspoon hot sauce (I prefer Tabasco due to the low salt content)
2 cups chicken broth or chicken bone broth
1 small zucchini, chopped
Cooked rice (optional)

1. In a medium-size mixing bowl combine the flour, salt, garlic, white pepper and cayenne.
2. Toss in the chicken pieces and coat each piece.
3. Heat 3 tablespoons of oil in a large skillet over medium-high heat. You want it hot enough to sizzle and turn the chicken strips a nice golden brown but not so hot that they'll burn easily.
4. Brown and set aside. The chicken doesn't have to be fully cooked at this time.
5. In a large pot add the onion and the remaining oil (1 tablespoon) and cook over medium-high heat for 3 min. or until the onions have softened.
6. Add the chopped fresh tomatoes, basil, hot sauce, chicken broth and fried chicken pieces along with oil and drippings to the pot of onions.
7. Bring the gumbo to a boil over high heat and then reduce to a medium rolling simmer for 15 minutes. Stir occasionally towards the end because it will begin to thicken.
8. Add the chopped zucchini and continue to cook for another 10 minutes.
9. Serve in individual serving bowls or on top of rice.

COOK'S NOTE
With okra so high in oxalates it made me sad to think I had to give up a perfectly delicious bowl of gumbo. With one little tweak, adding diced zucchini near the end of the cooking time, I was surprised to find it added that same texture you get with okra. I was pleased to put gumbo back on my table again. The total time to prepare and cook this meal may be more than my 30 minute time preference, but it is well worth the effort.

NUTRITIONAL INFORMATION
Calories 234 Carb 15g Fat 15g Protein 12g

LOADED BEEF BURGER
A thick vegetable puree adds both moisture and nutrients to these grass-fed beef burgers.

SERVES 4-6
INGREDIENTS

½ small zucchini, cut in 4 pieces
1 small red onion, quartered
½ small red or yellow sweet bell pepper, quartered
1 cup broccoli florets
2 garlic cloves
1 egg
1 pound ground grass-fed beef (or turkey, venison, bison)
¼ teaspoon salt
Hamburger buns (I prefer Tapioca Buns)

1. Preheat oven to 375 degrees.
2. Puree the zucchini, onion, red sweet bell pepper, broccoli and garlic in a food processor or blender.
3. In a large bowl combine the pureed vegetable and remaining ingredients.
4. Form patties (6) and place on a large baking sheet with raised sides, to keep any juices from spilling over into the oven. Unlike a traditional burger these will not shrink up very much so you will want to shape them bun size.
5. Bake uncovered for 25-30 minutes or until meat is no longer pink.
6. Serve on buns with your favorite toppings.

COOK'S NOTE
Baked, fried, or grilled, these vegetable loaded burgers are delicious and highly nutritious. They are a good source of calcium, zinc, and vitamin B6.

NUTRITIONAL INFORMATION
Calories 274 Carbohydrate 6g Fat 17g Protein 26 g

FISH FRITTERS WITH SWEET & SPICY SAUCE
These savory fish fritters are paired smartly with a sweet and spicy dipping sauce.

SERVES 2-4
INGREDIENTS

Fish Fritters:
1 package (12 ounces) fresh or frozen, wild-caught mahi mahi fish fillets, thawed
½ cup water
1 teaspoon lemon juice
½ cup cornmeal, plain
¼ cup flour, all purpose
1 teaspoon baking powder
1 teaspoon dried thyme
½ teaspoon salt
½ teaspoon cayenne pepper
¼ teaspoon garlic powder
2 eggs, lightly beaten
2 tablespoons lemon juice
¼ medium red onion, finely chopped
¼ red bell pepper, finely chopped
3 tablespoons milk
½ cup unrefined coconut oil or ghee
1 avocado, sliced (optional)
1 tomato, sliced (optional)

Sweet and Spicy Sauce:
½ cup apricot jam
2 tablespoons water
3 tablespoons Dijon mustard
2 tablespoons lemon juice

½ teaspoon cayenne pepper
¼ teaspoon dried ginger
¼ teaspoon red pepper flakes
¼ teaspoon onion powder

1. Make the sweet and spicy sauce by adding all of the ingredients together. Mix well and set aside.
2. In a large skillet, simmer the fish in the water and lemon juice over high heat, for about 6 minutes, until the fish flakes easily. Drain and flake the fish into chunks then set aside.
3. In a large mixing bowl, combine the cornmeal, flour, baking powder, thyme, salt, cayenne and garlic. Mix well.
4. In another mixing bowl, lightly beat the eggs then add the lemon juice, onion, pepper and milk.
5. Add the wet ingredients to the dry ingredients and stir in the cooked fish. (Mix together really well.)
6. Heat oil in large skillet over medium-high heat. Form small (1 ½ inch) balls using a teaspoon and the palm of your hand and drop fritter mix in the hot oil.
7. Cook 1-2 minutes per side or until golden brown and drain on paper towels.
8. Serve fish fritters with the dipping sauce on the side and the sliced avocado and tomato if desired.

COOK'S NOTE
It's hard to imagine these super delicious fried fish fritters as healthy, but unlike typical restaurant fritters these are fried in unrefined coconut oil which promotes heart health, supports immune function, and helps maintain normal blood sugar levels.

NUTRITIONAL INFORMATION
Calories 359 Carbohydrate 30g Fat 16g Protein 23g

PASTA PRIMAVERA

A light, meatless, colorful pasta dish loaded with fresh vegetables and rich flavor.

SERVES 4
INGREDIENTS

Angel hair pasta (8 ounces) cooked according to package directions
1 medium red onion, sliced thinly
2 tablespoons butter, divided
½ cup white wine
3 garlic cloves, chopped
½ teaspoon salt
1 bunch (20-25 spears) asparagus, tough ends trimmed and cut into 1 inch pieces
½ zucchini, chopped
¼ cup olive oil
1 roma tomato, diced
½ teaspoon fresh basil, chopped
4 tablespoons black olives, drained and sliced
½ cup parmesan cheese, grated or shredded

1. While the water for the pasta is coming to a boil stir-fry the onion in 1 tablespoon butter in a large skillet until soft.
2. Add the white wine, garlic, salt, and asparagus and cook for 4 minutes over medium heat. (This would be a good time to add the pasta to the boiling water.)
3. Add the zucchini and continue to cook for another 2 minutes.
4. Add the olive oil, 1 tablespoon butter, tomatoes, basil and olives and cook 2 minutes more.
5. Serve the garden mixture over the angel hair pasta and top with parmesan cheese.

COOK'S NOTE
This super quick dish delivers 83% of your daily requirement of vitamin K. Vitamin K works with calcium and vitamin D to help move calcium into bones and teeth where it belongs instead of other areas of the body. It also keeps blood vessels from calcifying.

NUTRITIONAL INFORMATION
Calories 563 Carbohydrate 51g Fat 29g Protein 21g

HERBED SALMON AND CREAM PEAS

Salmon with lavish sprinklings of mouthwatering spices served over a simple but elegant bed of creamy, colorful peas and corn.

SERVES 2-4
INGREDIENTS

1 pound wild-caught Alaskan salmon filets, fresh or frozen and thawed.
1 tablespoon butter
2 tablespoons Dijon mustard
½ teaspoon basil
½ teaspoon chives
½ teaspoon dried thyme
½ teaspoon dill weed
½ teaspoon garlic powder
½ teaspoon white pepper
¼ teaspoon salt
1 tablespoon butter
1 cup frozen sweet peas
1 cup frozen sweet corn
¾ cup whole milk
1 garlic clove, crushed
1 teaspoon dried thyme

1. Preheat oven to 425 degrees.
2. Place salmon in a buttered 9" x 13" baking pan or dish, skin side down.
3. Coat each salmon fillet with Dijon mustard.
4. Combine the basil, chives, thyme, dill weed, garlic, salt and pepper in a small bowl and sprinkle over the salmon filets.
5. Roast 15-18 minutes, without turning.
6. While the salmon fillets are cooking add the remaining ingredients to a medium-size saucepan and cook over medium-high heat (simmering) until cream is reduced by one-third and slightly thickened. This will take about 6-7 minutes after reaching a boil.
7. To serve, place a generous mound of creamy pea and corn in the middle of each plate. Spread it out so that it creates a bed for the salmon. Place a fillet of salmon on top.

COOK'S NOTE
The salmon seasonings are an excellent source of phytochemicals which fend off damaging free radicals. These salmon filets can be grilled in the summer months for an even greater flavor.

NUTRITIONAL INFORMATION
Calories 604 Carbohydrate 32g Fat 30g Protein 53g

MAHI MAHI WITH ARTICHOKE HEARTS
Packed full of flavor, this delicious fish dish is a meal in itself but can be accompanied by rice.

SERVES 2
INGREDIENTS

1 teaspoon red pepper flakes
¼ teaspoon salt
¼ teaspoon white pepper
1 ½ tablespoons all purpose flour
4 tablespoons butter (2 tablespoons for frying and 2 tablespoons added later)
1 package (12 ounces) fresh or frozen, wild-caught mahi mahi fish fillets, thawed and patted dry
Juice of ½ lemon
2 tablespoons heavy whipping cream
¼ teaspoon dried basil
1 garlic clove, minced
1 jar (12 ounces) artichoke hearts, drained and rinsed
1 jar (4-5 ounces) sun-dried tomatoes in olive oil, drained but not rinsed
Cooked rice (optional)

1. On a large plate add the red pepper flakes, salt, and pepper to the flour then spread it out on the plate.
2. In a large frying pan, melt 2 tablespoons butter over moderate heat.
3. Dust the fish with a small amount of flour and shake off any excess.
4. Cook fish on one side to a light golden brown (about 3-4 minutes) then turn and cook an additional 3-4 minutes lowering the heat to medium.
5. Add the remaining butter (2 tablespoons) lemon juice, heavy whipping cream, basil, and garlic.
6. Blend and spoon it over the fish. Then add the artichoke hearts and the sun-dried tomatoes.

7. Cook only a minute or two more stirring the artichokes and tomatoes into the lemon butter sauce.
8. Place the fish on plates, top with the artichoke hearts, tomatoes, and lemon butter sauce.
9. For a fuller meal serve over rice.

COOK'S NOTE
Grouper could be an alternative to mahi mahi as both of these fish are firm and flavorful. Each serving provides 41% of your daily requirements for B6 and magnesium.

NUTRITIONAL INFORMATION
Calories 642 Carbohydrate 43g Fat 37g Protein 42g

GREEK BAKED FISH
Greek style baked cod with a few spices and a mixture of lemon juice, olive oil, and garlic.

SERVES 4
INGREDIENTS

3-4 fresh or frozen, wild-caught cod fish fillets or any mild white fish
1 tablespoon lemon juice
1 ½ tablespoons olive oil
2 garlic cloves, minced
2 tablespoons red bell pepper, diced
2 tablespoons red onion, minced
1 tablespoon black olives, chopped
Salt and white pepper as desired.

1. Preheat oven to 400 degrees.
2. Line a baking sheet with parchment paper and place fish on it.
3. Drizzle lemon juice and the olive oil over fish.
4. Sprinkle with the garlic, bell pepper, and onion.
5. Season with a little salt and pepper.
6. Bake for 10-12 minutes.
7. Spoon the pan juices over the top of the fish and serve.

COOK'S NOTE
If you're looking for interesting, delicious, healthy ways to cook fish on a weeknight, this could be for you. Excellent served with a Greek salad.

NUTRITIONAL INFORMATION
Calories 295 Carbohydrate 3.6g Fat 18.4g Protein 28.6g

SALMON PASTA CASSEROLE
A rich and hearty meal full of calcium and omega-3 fatty acids.

SERVES 4
INGREDIENTS

3 cups cooked (according to package directions) rice noodles (I prefer Pad Thai Rice Noodles)
1 cup broccoli florets
1 cup frozen sweet peas
1 can (14 ounces) wild-caught Alaskan salmon, drained
2 eggs
1 tablespoon lemon juice
2 medium green onions
1 cup plain whole milk yogurt or sour cream
1 cup cheddar cheese, shredded

1. Preheat oven to 350 degrees.
2. Cook rice noodles according to package directions along with the broccoli florets and peas.
3. Drain the pasta, peas, and broccoli and set aside.
4. In a large mixing bowl, flake the salmon and mix it with the eggs and lemon juice; and then stir in the green onions, yogurt, and cheese.
5. Lightly oil a 9x13 casserole dish.
6. Layer the dish with the cooked pasta, peas, and broccoli and top with salmon mix.
7. Bake for 20 minutes. It will start to bubble round the edges and turn a golden color. You don't want to let it go too dark, the fish will overcook.

COOK'S NOTE
Pad Thai noodles are a great replacement for wheat pasta in this salmon pasta casserole. The texture and flavor are very similar. Canned salmon is calcium rich, provides high quality protein, and is an omega-3 powerhouse.

NUTRITIONAL INFORMATION ·
Calories 469 Carbohydrate 45g Fat 19g Protein 29g

SLOW COOKER INDIAN CHICKEN
A simple yet exquisite Indian dish. In India this is traditionally made with goat meat. Lamb or pork would work as well, but chicken is preferred in my home.

SERVES 4-6
INGREDIENTS

1 red onion, thinly sliced
½ red bell pepper, chopped
3 garlic cloves, thinly sliced
2 boneless chicken breasts
1 head napa cabbage, chopped
½ teaspoon ginger
1 teaspoon curry powder
¼ teaspoon cayenne pepper
¼ teaspoon white pepper
¼ teaspoon salt
1 can (13 ounces) coconut milk
1½ cups chicken broth
Cooked rice

1. Spread the onions, red bell pepper, and garlic around the bottom of the slow cooker.
2. Place the chicken over the onion mix.
3. Add the chopped cabbage and the 5 seasonings.
4. Pour the coconut milk and the chicken broth over the cabbage and with a large spoon press down the ingredients.
5. Cook on high for 4-6 hours.
6. Using two forks shred the chicken and mix the ingredients.
7. Serve over rice.

COOK'S NOTE
All of the flavors come through in a balanced way in this slow approach to making a traditional Indian dish that includes curry powder. Research suggests curry powder may help remove metals like lead and mercury from the body.

NUTRITIONAL INFORMATION
Calories 359 Carbohydrate 13g Fat 20g Protein 34g

SLOW COOKER UNSTUFFED CABBAGE
Easy, delicious, healthy, and without all of the work that goes into making the traditional stuffed cabbage roll.

SERVES 4
INGREDIENTS

1 pound ground grass-fed beef (or turkey, venison, bison)
1 cup uncooked rice
1 medium red onion, finely chopped
1 medium red or yellow pepper, finely chopped
I medium green or purple cabbage, chopped
4 roma tomatoes, chopped
1 jar tomato or spaghetti sauce (I prefer Eden Organic or Muir Glen)
½ cup water
1 teaspoon salt
½ teaspoon white pepper

1. Stir-fry the beef over medium-high heat and add to the slow cooker.
2. Add the remaining ingredients to the slow cooker in the order written.
3. Cook on low for 6-8 hours or on high for 3-4 hours.
4. Stir the pot and serve hot.

COOK'S NOTE
Cabbage is a superfood chock-full of antioxidants and sulfur-based compounds called glucosinolates, which protects one from developing a leaky gut. A leaky gut has been linked to oxalate issues in the body.

NUTRITIONAL INFORMATION
Calories 579 Carbohydrate 75g Fat 18g Protein 31g

STEAK & BRUSSELS SPROUT HASH

An elegant but simple meal with skillet seared ribeye steak, Brussels sprouts, and potatoes.

SERVES 2
INGREDIENTS

2 red potatoes, peeled and cut in chunks
6 ounces fresh or thawed Brussels sprouts
1 medium red onion, chopped
2 garlic cloves, sliced
2 tablespoons butter
2 small ribeye steaks
½ teaspoon salt
½ teaspoon white pepper
¼ cup dry white wine such as Pinot Grigio

1. In a medium-size saucepan cover them with water and bring to a boil. Reduce to medium heat and simmer until tender when pierced (7-8 minutes). Drain and set aside when done.
2. While the potatoes and Brussels sprouts are cooking, chop the onion and slice the garlic and set aside.
3. Heat the butter in a large skillet over high heat.
4. Add salt and pepper to the dried steaks and sear both sides in the hot skillet.
5. Add the onion and garlic to the skillet; reduce to a medium-high heat and cover.
6. Cook covered, 2-3 minutes, until the onions have browned.
7. Remove the steaks to individual plates.
8. Add the drained Brussels sprouts, potatoes and the wine to the skillet and cook about 1 minute, stirring occasionally to scrape up any caramelized bits from bottom of pan.
9. Serve the hash over the seared ribeye steaks.

COOK'S NOTE

Brussels sprouts are one of the world's healthiest foods. They are a good source of iron, potassium, and folate. Brussels sprouts pair well with beef due to the high levels of other B vitamins in the beef. B vitamins work together to release energy from food.

NUTRITIONAL INFORMATION
Calories 606 Carbohydrate 42g Fat 21g Protein 57g

SWEET AND SPICY STIR-FRY

A quick and easy stir-fry with a delicate sweet flavor.

SERVES 2
INGREDIENTS

2 tablespoons coconut oil or ghee
½ red onion, thinly sliced
½ red bell pepper, thinly sliced
1 large boneless chicken breast filet, cut into ¾ inch pieces
2 garlic cloves, crushed
¼ teaspoon dried ginger
½ teaspoon cayenne pepper
½ teaspoon white pepper
1 head Chinese (napa or savoy) cabbage
4 tablespoons rice wine (may substitute with any dry white wine)
¼ cup apricot jam
Cooked rice (optional)

1. Heat the wok or skillet over high heat then add the oil.
2. When the oil is heated, add onion and bell pepper and cook until tender.
3. Add the chicken and stir-fry for about 3 minutes.
4. Season with garlic, ginger, cayenne, and white pepper.
5. Add the cabbage and continue to stir-fry, about 8 minutes, until it starts to brown and stick to the skillet.
6. Reduce the heat to medium-high. Add the wine and the apricot jam and stir-fry for another minute to blend the flavors.
7. Transfer to a serving dish and serve hot or over cooked rice for a fuller meal.

COOK'S NOTE

Stir-frying is a fast, easy, and healthy way to cook. It's a good idea to measure and cut up ingredients before you heat the wok or skillet.

NUTRITIONAL INFORMATION
Calories 221 Carbohydrate 20g Fat 8g Protein 17g

LOW OXALATE BURRITO

Black-eyed peas create the tasty filling for an easy burrito.

Serves 6
INGREDIENTS

6 corn tortillas
2 cups cooked black-eyed peas
½ teaspoon garlic powder
2 spring onions, chopped
1 ½ teaspoons dried cumin
1 cup cheddar cheese, shredded

1. If serving immediately, preheat the oven to 200 degrees. Wrap the tortillas in some aluminum foil and let them heat up for about 15 minutes.
2. In a frying pan, add the black-eyed peas, garlic and a small splash of water. Cook on a medium heat for 1 minute, and then add in onion and cumin.
3. Continue to cook for a few minutes, until the beans are softened and moist. Partially mash them with a fork or masher so you have a chunky bean paste.
4. Remove the tortillas from the oven and place one on a plate. Spread about 3 tbsp of the bean mixture down the middle, top with cheese, and wrap.
5. Serve right away or cover with aluminum foil and freeze to reheat later.

COOK'S NOTE

A much healthier option than frozen burritos. Black-eyed peas are packed with protein and fiber.

NUTRITIONAL INFORMATION
Calories 190 Carbohydrate 22.7g Fat 7.5g Protein 9.9g

CRISPY GARLIC PARMESAN WINGS

Baked instead of fried but these classic chicken wings are crispy and delicious.

SERVES 2-4
INGREDIENTS

10-12 chicken wings
1 teaspoon salt
½ tsp white pepper
1 teaspoon garlic powder
1 teaspoon dried oregano
2 eggs beaten with a tablespoon of water
¾ cup parmesan cheese

1. Preheat the oven to 425 degrees.
2. Place the wings in a large bowl and season the with the salt, pepper, garlic powder and oregano.
3. Beat the eggs in a shallow bowl with 1 tablespoon of water.
4. Pour the eggs into the bowl of chicken and mix well.
5. Add in the parmesan cheese and coat the wings on all sides.
6. Place the chicken wings on a parchment lined baking sheet.
7. Bake for 25-30 minutes.

COOK'S NOTE

If your wings aren't golden and crispy after 30 minutes, turn the broiler on and broil them for about 3 more minutes, watching them carefully as they could burn quickly.

NUTRITIONAL INFORMATION
Calories 430 Carbohydrate 7g Fat 20.3 Protein 52

GLUTEN FREE PIZZA CRUST

A light and crispy crust that is quick and easy to make.

SERVES 4
INGREDIENTS

⅓ cup plus 2 tablespoons rice flour
⅓ cup plus 2 tablespoons cornmeal flour
1 teaspoon baking powder
½ teaspoon salt
3 cloves garlic, minced
1 egg, beaten
1 tablespoon olive oil
½ cup Parmigiano-Reggiano or cheddar cheese, shredded
⅔ cup water

1. Preheat oven to 450 degrees.
2. In a medium-size bowl, combine the rice flour, cornmeal, baking powder and salt.
3. In a separate bowl, mix the garlic, egg, olive oil, Parmigiano-Reggiano or cheddar cheese and water. Whisk well.
4. Add the wet ingredients to the dry and mix well.
5. Spread the mix over a parchment lined baking sheet and bake for 15 minutes.
6. Remove the crust from the oven and add your own choice of toppings. Bake an additional 10 minutes.
7. Slice and serve.

COOK'S NOTE

Because it is made with baking powder instead of yeast, this recipe requires no kneading or rising time, so you can have homemade pizza ready to serve in less than 30 minutes.

NUTRITIONAL INFORMATION
Calories 230 Carbohydrate 22g Fat 12.2g Protein 8g

WHITE CHICKEN CHILI

Enjoy a taste of the south with this delicious white chicken chili full of spice, chicken, and low oxalate black-eyed peas.

SERVES 2-4
INGREDIENTS

2 tablespoons olive oil
2 large chicken breasts, cut into bite-size pieces.
2 cloves garlic, chopped
½ red onion, diced
1 tablespoon dried oregano
1 tablespoon dried cumin
½ tablespoon dried thyme
½ tablespoon dried basil
½ teaspoon salt
1 teaspoon white pepper
4 ½ cups black-eyed peas
1 cup water
1 cup sour cream
4 ounces cream cheese

1. Heat olive oil in a large pot over medium heat and add chicken, garlic, onion, oregano, cumin, thyme, basil, salt, and pepper.
2. Cook and stir until juices run clear, 5 to 8 minutes. Stir in the cooked black-eyed peas and water.
3. Reduce heat to medium-low and simmer, stirring occasionally, until flavors combine, about 10 minutes.
4. Stir in the sour cream and cheese and simmer until thick, about 25 minutes.
5. Ladle into bowls.

COOK'S NOTE
Black-eyed peas are mild, flavorful, and full of protein. One cup of black-eyed peas is low in fat, cholesterol-free and provides more than 30% of the daily recommended amount of fiber.

NUTRITIONAL INFORMATION
Calories 250 Carbohydrate 30g Fat 10g Protein 31.9g

GLAZED SALMON

Glazed salmon with a perfectly balanced sweet and savory flavor.

SERVES 2
INGREDIENTS

3 tablespoons butter or ghee
5 tablespoons honey
1 tablespoon lemon juice
1 garlic clove, minced
¼ teaspoon salt
¼ teaspoon white pepper'
2 tablespoons bourbon (optional)
1 can (14 ounces) wild-caught Alaskan Salmon

1. Melt the butter or ghee in a large skillet; then add all of the ingredients except the salmon. Cook over medium heat for about 1 minute.
2. Add in the salmon and break it up into bite size chunks. Toss until the salmon is coated in the sauce.
3. Serve as a main dish. Other options include serving over rice or wrapped with a flour tortilla.

COOK'S NOTE
Similar to other oily fish like tuna or trout, salmon is rich in omega-3 fatty acids.

NUTRITIONAL INFORMATION
Calories 636 Carbohydrate 45g Fat 32.3g Protein 44g

SALMON PESTO PASTA

A fresh and wholesome Mediterranean-inspired dish that's perfect for a quick and healthy meal.

SERVES 2
INGREDIENTS

8 ounces penne pasta
1 cup packed fresh basil leaves
⅓ cup parmesan cheese, grated
¼ cup olive oil
3 cloves garlic, chopped
1 teaspoon onion powder
½ tablespoon squeezed lemon juice
Salt and pepper to taste
1 cup frozen green peas
1 can (6 ounces) wild-caught Alaskan salmon, drained

1. Cook pasta according to package directions in a pot of lightly salted water. Drain and set aside.
2. While pasta is cooking: Place basil leaves, cheese, olive oil, garlic, onion powder, lemon juice and salt and pepper in a food processor. Pulse until smooth.
3. Split cooked pasta between two plates. Top with pesto, peas, and salmon.
4. Garnish with additional parmesan cheese and serve.

COOK'S NOTE
Spiralized zucchini can replace the pasta making the recipe gluten-free.

NUTRITIONAL INFORMATION
Calories 546   Carbohydrates 14g   Fat 42g   Protein 28g

SLOW COOKER THAI CHICKEN THIGHS

This Thai chicken recipe is perfectly spiced and incredibly tender.

SERVES 4
INGREDIENTS

2 teaspoons coconut oil, olive oil or ghee
4 tablespoons honey
7 tablespoons white wine vinegar
1 tablespoon molasses
1 teaspoon salt
½ teaspoon white pepper
¼ teaspoon garlic powder
¼ teaspoon onion powder
⅛ teaspoon dried ginger
⅛ teaspoon dried cilantro
8 chicken thighs

1. Oil the bottom of the slow cooker with the oil.
2. Combine all of the following ingredients except the chicken in a bowl and mix well.
3. Add the chicken and toss to coat.
4. Pour all of the ingredients into the slow cooker and cook on low for 6-8 hours.

COOK'S NOTE

Using chicken thighs allows you to cook it longer (6-8 hours on low) without drying out if you will be away all day. I recommend boneless, skinless thighs for this since the skin would add a lot of rendered fat to the sauce.

NUTRITIONAL INFORMATION
Calories 523 Carbohydrate 22g Fat 26.2g Protein 47g

MAHI MAHI FISH TACOS

Light, fresh seasoned fish tacos with a fruity, sweet and spicy Caribbean slaw.

SERVES 4-6
INGREDIENTS

Slaw:
2 cups savoy cabbage, shredded
2 tablespoons Dijon mustard
1 tablespoon honey
2 tablespoons white wine vinegar or lemon juice
1 teaspoon garlic, minced
1 teaspoon Tabasco sauce
2 tablespoons olive oil
3 tablespoons apricot jam
2 tablespoons plain whole milk yogurt or sour cream
Salt and pepper as desired

Fish:
¼ teaspoon salt
¼ teaspoon garlic powder
¼ teaspoon onion powder
½ teaspoon dried cilantro
¼ teaspoon cumin
¼ teaspoon white pepper
1 package (12 ounces) fresh or frozen, wild-caught mahi mahi fish fillets, thawed and patted dry
2 tablespoons butter or ghee
4-6 corn or flour tortillas
Avocado slices, optional
Sour cream, optional
Tomato, optional
Salsa, optional

1. Add all of the first 9 ingredients for the slaw to a large mixing bowl and whisk together until fully combined.
2. Add in the cabbage and toss well to combine.
3. Refrigerate slaw while preparing the mahi mahi fish.
4. Combine the salt, garlic, onion, cilantro, cumin and white pepper in a small bowl.

5. Slice the mahi mahi fillets lengthwise and sprinkle the spice mix evenly over each filet, rubbing it on all sides.
6. In a skillet set over medium-high heat, heat the butter or ghee and add the mahi mahi fillets.
7. Cook, undisturbed until they're just beginning to blacken, about 4 minutes. Flip the fish and cook for another 3 minutes. Transfer to a plate.
8. Warm the tortillas according to package directions.
9. Divide the fish among the warm tortillas and top it with the slaw. Optional toppings include avocado slices, sour cream, chopped tomato, or even salsa.

COOK'S NOTE
I used mahi mahi in this fish taco recipe because it's light and has a mild flavor, but still has a hearty texture.

NUTRITIONAL INFORMATION
Calories 263 Carbohydrate 35g Fat 13.1g Protein 4g

CAJUN COD BAKE
The bold spices give the mild cod a perfect kick of flavor.

SERVES 4
INGREDIENTS

2 medium red potatoes, peeled and sliced about ¼ inch
1 medium onion, sliced thin
2 garlic cloves, chopped
3 tablespoons olive oil
¼ teaspoon salt
⅛ teaspoon white pepper
3-4 wild-caught (fresh or frozen) cod fish fillets
½ teaspoon oregano
¼ teaspoon dried thyme
¼ cup butter, melted

1. Preheat oven to 375 degrees.
2. In a large bowl combine the first 6 ingredients and mix well.
3. Spread in a casserole dish and bake 20 minutes.
4. Remove from the oven and place the codfish fillets on top and season with oregano and thyme.
5. Drizzle the melted butter evenly over the top.
6. Return dish to the oven and bake 15 minutes more.

COOK'S NOTE
You can scoop the fish out into a bowl and then put the pan back in the oven if the potatoes aren't quite done when the fish is. Just cover them and add them back in once the potatoes are done.

NUTRITIONAL INFORMATION
Calories 485 Carbohydrate 30g Fat 31.2g Protein 22g

SALMON WITH MUSTARD CREAM

Simple ingredients come together for an easy, tasty meal of salmon with a sweet and savory sauce over the top.

SERVES 4
INGREDIENTS

4 wild-caught salmon fillets, skin on
1 cup heavy whipping cream
1 tablespoon Dijon mustard
1 tablespoon chives, chopped
Salt and pepper as desired

1. Preheat oven to 400 degrees.
2. Place the salmon fillets skin-side-down on a parchment paper-lined baking sheet.
3. Bake the salmon fillets for 10 to 15 minutes.
4. While the salmon is baking, combine the cream and the mustard in a small saucepan. Stir over low heat until the sauce is warmed-through and has thickened slightly.
5. Remove the fillets from the parchment paper with a spatula and place on dinner plates.
6. Spoon the mustard cream sauce over each salmon fillet.
7. Sprinkle the chives over the sauced salmon fillets.
8. Season to taste with salt and pepper.

COOK'S NOTE

Another variation is to replace the Dijon mustard with honey mustard.

NUTRITIONAL INFORMATION
Calories 668 Carbohydrate 1g Fat 36.4g Protein 79g

JERK MAHI MAHI

Mahi mahi fish fillets pan fried with the spicy, sweet, and flavorful jerk seasonings of the Caribbean.

SERVES 4
INGREDIENTS

1 tablespoon allspice
1 teaspoon onion powder
1 teaspoon ground ginger
½ teaspoon white pepper
½ teaspoon dried thyme
½ teaspoon salt
¼ teaspoon nutmeg
1 teaspoon cayenne pepper
4 fresh or frozen, wild-caught mahi mahi fish fillets
2 tablespoons coconut oil or ghee

1. Mix the first 8 spices in a small bowl.
2. Coat the mahi mahi filets in the spices.
3. Pan fry the filets until cooked throughout with a white and flaky texture, approximately 5-7 min per side.

COOK'S NOTE

Coconut oil adds to the tropical theme, but olive oil, butter, or ghee will do. Use your remaining jerk seasoning on any side you add.

NUTRITIONAL INFORMATION
Calories 308 Carbohydrate 2g Fat 9.7g Protein 50g

CHICKEN MARSALA

Pan seared chicken tied together with the flavors of a creamy mushroom and marsala wine sauce

SERVES 6
INGREDIENTS

1 tablespoon olive oil
6 boneless skinless chicken breasts
salt and pepper to taste
1 ½ cups sliced mushrooms
2 teaspoons minced garlic
¼ cup marsala wine
½ cup chicken or bone broth
¼ cup heavy cream

1. Heat the olive oil in a large pan over medium-high heat.
2. Season the chicken with salt and pepper on both sides. Add the chicken to the pan and cook for 5-6 minutes on each side or until cooked through.
3. Remove the chicken from the pan and cover with foil to keep warm.
4. Add the mushrooms to the pan and cook for 4-5 minutes or until tender.
5. Add the garlic and cook for an additional 30 seconds.
6. Add the marsala wine and chicken broth to the pan and simmer for 5 minutes.
7. Stir in the cream and simmer for 2 more minutes. Add the chicken back to the pan and spoon the sauce over the top and serve.

COOK'S NOTE
Make sure to cook off the alcohol in the wine, so you're only getting the flavor from the Marsala. You'll know that the alcohol has evaporated when you can't smell it anymore.

NUTRITIONAL INFORMATION
Calories 242 Carbohydrate 8g Fat 25g Protein 25g

FLOUNDER WITH LEMON BUTTER

Quick, and elegant flounder covered in a lemon butter sauce.

SERVES 4
INGREDIENTS

4 fresh flounder fillets (or substitute any white fish)
½ teaspoon salt
¼ teaspoon white pepper
2 tablespoons olive oil
3 tablespoons butter
Juice of 1 lemon
2 tablespoons basil

1. Pat both sides of the fish fillets dry with paper towels and then season them with salt and pepper.
2. Heat the oil in a medium skillet over medium-high heat until the oil ripples but isn't smoking.
3. Add the fillets to the skillet and cook, without moving, for 2 minutes. Slide a thin metal spatula underneath the fillets and carefully flip each one. If it seems impossible to slip the spatula beneath the fillet and the skillet, remove the skillet from the heat and wait 30 seconds or so and try again.
4. Place a slice of butter on top of each fish fillet and stand idly by as it melts and drips off the fish into the skillet. Cook the fish about 2 minutes more.
5. Use a spatula to transfer the fish to a platter.
6. Squeeze the lemon juice into the skillet and with the skillet still over the heat, use a wooden spoon to scrape up any browned bits stuck to the bottom of the skillet. Stir in the fresh basil and spoon the sauce over the fish. Serve.

COOK'S NOTE

Flour isn't at all essential for a lovely sear on fish. Just use a good stainless steel pan that's lightly oiled.

NUTRITIONAL INFORMATION
Calories 253 Carbohydrate 1g Fat 18.6g Protein 20g

ITALIAN SALMON BAKE

A delicious, hearty, and easy to prepare salmon topped with blanched romaine and parmesan cheese.

SERVES 4
INGREDIENTS

1 cup romaine lettuce, chopped
¼ cup heavy cream
½ cup parmesan cheese, grated
1 teaspoon nutmeg
4 wild-caught Alaskan salmon fillets

1. Preheat oven to 400 degrees.
2. Blanch romaine by placing in boiling water for 30 seconds then drain and rinse.
3. Squeeze out excess liquid and chop finely.
4. In a small bowl combine romaine, cream, parmesan cheese, and nutmeg.
5. Place salmon, skin side down, on a non-stick or parchment lined baking sheet.
6. Bake until salmon is cooked through, about 12 to 15 minutes.
7. Remove from the oven and top with cheese and romaine mixture.
8. Return to the oven and cook until golden.

COOK'S NOTE

A thin piece of salmon might only need about 10-12 minutes in the oven at this temperature, while a thicker piece of fish may require 15-18 minutes.

NUTRITIONAL INFORMATION
Calories 646 Carbohydrate 3g Fat 31.6g Protein 82g

SLOW COOKER CHICKEN AND WILD RICE

A delicious, rich and easy, one-dish slow cooker casserole of chicken and wild rice that absorbs the flavors of all of the ingredients.

SERVES 4
INGREDIENTS

2 tablespoons butter or ghee
1 ¼ cups wild rice
4 boneless skinless chicken thighs or breasts
2 garlic cloves, minced
1 red onion, chopped
½ teaspoon salt
¼ teaspoon white pepper
3 cups water

1. Generously oil the slow cooker with butter.
2. In a fine mesh strainer, rinse the wild rice blend to remove excess starch. Add to the slow cooker.
3. If using chicken breasts, cut each breast into 2-3 even pieces. Add chicken to the slow cooker.
4. Add in the minced garlic, onion, seasonings, and then the water.
5. Cover and cook on high for 4 hours or until the chicken is cooked through, rice is tender, and most of the liquid has been absorbed.

COOK'S NOTE

Unfortunately, this casserole doesn't do well on low settings in the slow cooker as the rice ends up very unevenly cooked. At the high setting there will be variation in times since every crockpot is different.

NUTRITIONAL INFORMATION
Calories 483 Carbohydrate 41g Fat 11.5g   Protein 56g

CHICKEN AND ARTICHOKES

This quick and easy skillet chicken dinner features artichokes and olives giving it a Greek flair.

SERVES 4
INGREDIENTS

4 boneless skinless chicken breast halves
¼ teaspoon salt
¼ teaspoon white pepper
3 teaspoons olive oil
1 jar (14 ounces) quartered artichoke hearts, rinsed and drained
⅔ cup water
¼ cup black olives, halved
1 teaspoon dried oregano
2 garlic cloves, minced
1 tablespoon lemon juice

1. Sprinkle chicken with salt and pepper. In a large skillet, heat oil over medium-high heat and brown chicken on both sides.
2. Add remaining ingredients and bring to a boil. Reduce heat and simmer covered, for about 5-7 minutes.

COOK'S NOTE
The artichokes hearts can be fresh, frozen and thawed, or packed in water in a jar. Whichever type you use, rinse them well.

NUTRITIONAL INFORMATION
Calories 225 Carbohydrate 9g Fat 9g Protein 26g

SUSHI BOWL
A simplified way to enjoy all the flavors of a sushi roll in a fraction of the time.

SERVES 2
INGREDIENTS

1 avocado
1 large cucumber
4 ounces cream cheese
2 dried seaweed sheets, also known as Nori
2 cups white rice, cooked
1 teaspoon lemon juice or white wine vinegar
¼ teaspoon salt

1. Chop your avocado and cucumber into small bite-size pieces.
2. Cut your cream cheese into strips.
3. Cut or tear the seaweed into small pieces.
4. Once you have everything prepared assemble the bowls in layers. Start with a layer of rice, add the seaweed, more rice, lemon juice or vinegar, cheese, avocado, and then cucumber.
5. Season with salt and serve.

COOK'S NOTE
The thin seaweed sheets (called Nori) that are used in making sushi are rich in protein, fiber, omega-3 fatty acids, and many vitamins and minerals. One sheet of Nori contains the same amount of fiber as a cup of spinach and is loaded in iodine, a mineral essential for proper hormone function. Nori is also high in calcium, magnesium, iron, Vitamin A, and Vitamin C.

NUTRITIONAL INFORMATION
Calories 578 Carbohydrate 59g Fat 34.8g Protein 11g

BAKED EGGS AND ASPARAGUS

Eggs with parmesan cheese baked over a bed of asparagus.

SERVES 4
INGREDIENTS

3 tablespoons olive oil
1 bunch asparagus, trimmed and cut into ½ -inch pieces
2 scallions, thinly sliced
6 large eggs
¼ teaspoon dried basil
¼ teaspoon cilantro
½ teaspoon salt
¼ teaspoon white pepper
⅓ cup heavy cream
2 tablespoons parmesan, grated

1. Heat the oven to 300 degrees.
2. In a large oven safe skillet over medium heat, warm the olive oil until shimmering. Add the asparagus and the scallions and cook for 5 minutes, stirring occasionally, until asparagus is browned and tender.
3. Whisk together the eggs, basil, cilantro, salt, pepper, and cream.
4. Whisk in parmesan and pour the egg mixture over asparagus.
5. Transfer the skillet to the oven and bake for about 20 minutes, until set.
6. Cool in the pan for about 10 minutes before serving. It is best warm, not hot.

COOK'S NOTE

Avoid canned asparagus; fresh tastes much better. Make sure your spears are bright green and have tightly closed tips. If you're cooking with purple or white asparagus, make sure it's a vivid purple or a bright white.

NUTRITIONAL INFORMATION
Calories 239 Carbohydrate 6g Fat 21.4g Protein 7g

SLOW COOKER BEEF STEW

A full-bodied beef stew that is so simple yet incredibly delicious.

SERVES 4
INGREDIENTS

1 tablespoon butter
1 pound grass-fed beef stew meat, cut in 2 inch chunks
½ cup carrots, sliced thick
2 red skinned potatoes, peeled and quartered
1 onion, chopped
1 large tomato, chopped
1 ½ cup fresh or frozen green peas
1 teaspoon salt
1 teaspoon dried rosemary
½ teaspoon thyme
½ teaspoon pepper
2 tablespoons tapioca flour
½ cup red wine
2 cups chicken broth, bone broth or water

1. Spread the butter in the bottom of the slow cooker, add all of the ingredients, and mix well.
2. Cook on low for 8-10 hours or on high for 4-5 hours.
3. Serve in individual soup bowls.

COOK'S NOTE
It's unnecessary to be sure the liquid covers all of the ingredients in a slow cooker since the condensation continually rains down on the ingredients. This will be the easiest and tastiest beef stew you've ever cooked. Tapioca flour is a gluten-free thickening agent. It thickens at low temperatures and has a neutral taste, so it won't compete with other flavors.

NUTRITIONAL INFORMATION
Calories 571 Carbohydrate 65g Fat 17g Protein 35g

SLOW COOKER MEATLOAF

Moist with mixed vegetables, this meatloaf still retains its shape in the slow cooker. The meat juices mingle with the potatoes making them absolutely delicious.

SERVES 4-6
INGREDIENTS

½ head cauliflower florets
½ red or yellow bell pepper, quartered
½ teaspoon salt
½ teaspoon white pepper
1 garlic clove
1 red onion, chopped
1 cup pumpkin puree
2 eggs, slightly beaten
1 pound ground grass-fed beef (or turkey, venison, bison)
Ketchup, as desired (avoid ketchup that contains high fructose corn syrup)
Fresh chopped basil, as garnish

1. Using a food processor or blender, add cauliflower, red or yellow bell pepper, salt, pepper, and garlic. Process until the ingredients are pureed.
2. In a large bowl, combine the pureed vegetables, chopped onion, pumpkin, eggs, and ground beef. Mix well.
3. Tear off a sheet of aluminum foil large enough to cover the bottom and sides of the slow cooker and place in the cooker. Not only will it help you shape a good loaf, but it will make removing it easier.
4. Spoon the loaf into the slow cooker and shape by gathering the aluminum foil ends and bouncing it a bit.
5. Top the meatloaf with ketchup, as desired.
6. Cover and cook on high for 6-8 hours.
7. Easily remove the meatloaf by lifting the aluminum foil, and transfer it to a serving dish.
8. Garnish with chopped fresh basil and serve.

COOK'S NOTE
This fabulous vegetable loaded meatloaf is a good source of vitamin B6, B12, and zinc.

NUTRITIONAL INFORMATION
Calories 419 Carbohydrate 8g Fat 32g Protein 28g

SNACKS AND SWEETS

CHEDDAR CRISPS
Crunchy cheese thins packed with flavor.

SERVES 1 (Makes 10-12)
INGREDIENTS

1 cup sharp cheddar cheese, shredded
⅛ teaspoon salt
⅛ teaspoon white pepper
¼ teaspoon onion powder
¼ teaspoon garlic powder

1. Preheat oven to 425 degrees and line a large baking sheet with parchment paper. You can oil the baking sheet first so that the parchment paper lies flat.
2. Drop large spoonfuls of cheese onto the sheet leaving about an inch of space between them. Flatten them out.
3. Mix the seasoning in a small bowl and sprinkle over each of the mounds.
4. Bake for about 7 minutes, until they melt completely but have not changed color.
5. Allow to cool before transferring to a serving dish.

COOK'S NOTE
Going gluten-free doesn't have to mean cracker-free. These simple cheese crisps make a light crunchy snack or a great garnish for any dish.

NUTRITIONAL INFORMATION
Calories 44 Carbohydrate 0g Fat 4g Protein 3g

PIZZA CRISPS

Crunchy Italian spiced parmesan cheese thins topped with tomato and olive.

SERVES 4
INGREDIENTS

1 cup parmesan cheese, shredded
⅛ teaspoon salt
⅛ teaspoon white pepper
⅛ teaspoon onion powder
⅛ teaspoon garlic powder
½ teaspoon dried Italian seasonings
1 tomato, sliced thin
Black olives, sliced (as desired)

1. Preheat oven to 400 degrees.
2. Line a large baking sheet with parchment paper. You can oil the baking sheet first so that the parchment paper will lie flat.
3. Drop large spoonfuls of cheese onto the sheet leaving about an inch of space between each. Flatten them out. (Makes 10-12)
4. Add the seasonings to a small bowl, mix well, and sprinkle over the cheese.
5. Bake in a hot oven for about 6-7 minutes or until they melt completely.
6. Allow to cool before transferring to a serving dish.
7. Top with a thin slice of tomato and olive slices just before serving.

COOK'S NOTE
These flavorful crispy thins make a great snack by themselves, but the addition of tomato and black olives transforms them into a tasty pizza-style appetizer.

NUTRITIONAL INFORMATION
Calories 248 Carbohydrate 4g Fat 16g Protein 22g

GUACAMOLE
Classically fresh avocado based dip made simple.

SERVES 2
INGREDIENTS

1 avocado
1 tablespoon red onion, minced
1 garlic clove, crushed
½ teaspoon lemon juice
1 tablespoon olive oil
2 dashes Tabasco sauce
Salt to taste
½ tablespoon cilantro

1. Halve your avocado and use a spoon to scoop the flesh out into a bowl.
2. Use a fork to mash up the avocado.
3. Squeeze in the lemon juice, add the onion, garlic, olive oil, hot sauce, salt, and cilantro and mix well.

COOK'S NOTE
In addition to its use in Mexican cuisine, it has become part of international and American cuisines as a dip, condiment, and salad ingredient. This foolproof recipe is perfect for a snack with veggies or on top of grilled chicken or burgers. Studies have shown that avocado extracts can significantly reduce symptoms of osteoarthritis.

NUTRITIONAL INFORMATION
Calories 227 Carbohydrate 3g Fat 22g Protein 9g

VEGETABLE CHEESE BALL
This tasty veggie-packed cream cheese ball can be made the night before serving.

SERVES 4-6
INGREDIENTS

16 ounces cream cheese
⅓ cup carrot, shredded
¼ cup red bell pepper, diced

¼ cup green onion, chopped
¼ cup black olives, chopped or sliced
¼ teaspoon salt
¼ teaspoon garlic powder
¼ cup pumpkin seeds, crushed

1. Allow cream cheese to soften slightly at room temperature.
2. While you let it soften, chop your veggies and crush your pumpkin seeds.
3. Add cream cheese to a large bowl and use a hand mixer to whip for about a minute. Add all your veggies, salt, and garlic powder and mix until veggies are dispersed throughout the cream cheese.
4. Spoon cream cheese onto a sheet of plastic wrap and form into a ball.
5. Refrigerate for a few minutes to set, if needed, then remove the plastic wrap.
6. Roll it in the crushed pumpkin seeds.
7. Serve with corn tortilla chips, rice crackers, sliced apple, or vegetables.

COOK'S NOTE
This vegetable cheese ball will keep in the fridge for 4-5 days.

NUTRITIONAL INFORMATION
Calories 291 Carbohydrate 5g Fat 28.3 Protein 6g

TUNA STUFFED EGGS
Tuna salad meets deviled eggs in this recipe for an appetizer or light lunch.

SERVES 4
INGREDIENTS

8 hard boiled eggs, halved
½ cup mayonnaise
1 (6 oz) can albacore tuna, packed in water, drained
1 tablespoon red onion, minced
2 teaspoons pickle juice
salt and pepper, to taste

1. In a small bowl combine the egg yolks with mayonnaise and mash.
2. Add tuna, red onion and pickle juice.
3. Scoop heaping spoonfuls of the tuna mix into the 16 halved eggs.

COOK'S NOTE
These hearty, flavor-packed French deviled eggs make a fantastic brunch, lunch, or appetizer.

NUTRITIONAL INFORMATION
Calories 296 Carbohydrate 4g Fat 20.6g Protein 23g

GREEN PEA HUMMUS
A fresh and flavorful alternative to traditional hummus.

SERVES 4
INGREDIENTS

1 tablespoon olive oil
½ cup chopped onion
2 cups green peas, fresh or frozen
¾ cup water
2 tablespoons fresh mint, chopped
2 tablespoons plain whole milk yogurt or sour cream
½ teaspoon salt
½ teaspoon white pepper

1. Heat the olive oil in a small pot over medium heat. Add the chopped onion and sauté until soft and translucent, but not browned, about 4-5 minutes.
2. Add the peas and water and bring to a boil.
3. Lower heat to medium and cook 5 minutes. Drain.
4. Add the peas and the remaining ingredients to a food processor and puree until smooth.
5. Serve chilled with carrots, cucumbers, bread, or tortilla chips for dipping.

COOK'S NOTE
Green peas are packed with protein, fiber, micronutrients, and are low in calories.

NUTRITIONAL INFORMATION
Calories 93 Carbohydrate 11g Fat 3.9g Protein 4g

FRIED SARDINES

Golden brown and crispy, these tender sardines are a tasty quick snack, appetizer or light lunch.

SERVES 2
INGREDIENTS

1 can (3-4 ounces) sardines, drained
1 egg
½ cup cornmeal
¼ teaspoon garlic powder
¼ teaspoon salt
½ teaspoon white pepper
¼ cup olive oil

1. Rinse and place the sardines on a paper towel to dry.
2. Beat the egg in a shallow bowl and set aside.
3. In another bowl, mix together the cornmeal, garlic powder, salt, and pepper.
4. Heat the olive oil in a large frying pan over medium heat.
5. Dip each sardine into the egg, then into the cornmeal to coat both sides and place in the frying pan.
6. Cook the sardines for about 3 minutes then turn and cook another 2-3 minutes.
7. Remove from the pan and place on a plate. (Do not place on a paper towel or they will lose their crispness). Serve.

COOK'S NOTE

Sardines are an excellent source of Vitamin B12, Omega 3, Vitamin D and calcium.

NUTRITIONAL INFORMATION
Calories 522 Carbohydrate 32g Fat 35.5g Protein 18g

APPLE MUFFINS

Deliciously soft and tender, moist muffins loaded with chunks of apple.

SERVES 12
INGREDIENTS

1 ¾ cups all purpose flour
1 ½ teaspoons baking powder
½ teaspoon nutmeg, dried
½ teaspoon salt
⅓ cup butter or ghee, melted
½ cup maple syrup
2 eggs, beaten
½ cup plain whole milk yogurt
1 teaspoon vanilla extract
1 ripe banana, mashed
2 apples, diced

1. Preheat oven to 400 degrees
2. Line a 12 cup muffin tin with paper muffin liners or use a non-stick silicone muffin pan.
3. In a large mixing bowl combine the flour, baking powder, nutmeg and salt.
4. In a separate bowl combine the butter, maple syrup, eggs, yogurt, and vanilla. Mix thoroughly.
5. Fold in the banana and apples, and then add to the flour. Stir until smooth.
6. Bake 16-20 minutes or until a toothpick inserted into center of a muffin comes out clean.

COOK'S NOTE
In a recipe like this, most of the sweetness will be based off your apple, so you will want to use a sweet apple. I used Honeycrisp because they're very sweet and I like the way they bake.

NUTRITIONAL INFORMATION
Calories 200 Carbohydrate 30g Fat 7.3g Protein 4g

COCONUT CAKE

A moist, protein and fiber rich cake made with coconut flour. It's just as healthy as it is delicious.

SERVES 10-12
INGREDIENTS

6 tablespoons coconut flour
½ teaspoon baking soda
¼ teaspoon salt
5 eggs
½ cup maple syrup
2 teaspoons vanilla
½ cup coconut oil, melted
½ cup unsweetened coconut, shredded
8 ounces cream cheese, softened
2 tablespoons butter, melted
¼ cup plain whole milk yogurt
1 teaspoon vanilla
1 cup maple syrup
1 cup unsweetened coconut, shredded

1. Preheat oven to 325 degrees.
2. Oil a 9x13 inch glass or ceramic baking dish.
3. Mix coconut flour, baking soda, and salt in a medium-size bowl.
4. In a separate bowl, add the eggs, syrup, vanilla, and coconut oil.
5. Pour the wet ingredients into the dry and mix well using an electric mixer on the lowest speed until very smooth.
6. Stir in the shredded coconut and pour the batter into the baking dish. Spread evenly.
7. Bake 35 minutes.
8. Use an electric mixer to blend all of the frosting ingredients until smooth. Then add 1 cup of coconut flakes and mix well with a spoon.
9. Allow the cake to cool before topping it with frosting.

COOK'S NOTE

It is easy to have variations of this cake. Simply replace the shredded coconut with fresh chopped strawberries or pineapple in both the cake and the frosting. The taste and texture is similar to a classic yellow cake.

NUTRITIONAL INFORMATION
Calories 651 Carbohydrate 44g Fat 52g Protein 7g

COCONUT CREAM SNOWBALLS

This creamy, crunchy, no bake coconut dessert is an all natural delight.

SERVES 6
INGREDIENTS

8 ounces cream cheese, softened
3 tablespoons honey
½ teaspoon vanilla
½ teaspoon coconut flour
1 cup unsweetened coconut, shredded

1. Combine the cream cheese, honey, vanilla and flour. Blend well.
2. Spread some shredded coconut out on a plate, drop a spoonful of batter onto the plate, and use both hands to shape the snowball as you coat with shredded coconut. Toss from hand to hand to remove excess coconut. Makes 12-14.
3. Repeat the process and add shredded coconut to the plate when needed.
4. Refrigerate for an hour before serving.

COOK'S NOTE
Eating healthy through the holidays can be a real challenge, but these fast and fabulous coconut cream snowballs satisfy that sweet craving without sacrificing your health.

NUTRITIONAL INFORMATION
Calories 438 Carbohydrate 20g Fat 40g Protein 6g

EASY CHEESECAKE

A moist and delicious cheesecake with a buttery, cookie-like, coconut flour crust.

SERVES 8
INGREDIENTS

Crust:
¾ cup coconut flour
¼ teaspoon salt
½ cup butter, melted
1 tablespoon honey
2 eggs

Filling:
½ cup honey
4 eggs
16 ounces cream cheese, softened
1 teaspoon vanilla
1½ cups plain whole milk yogurt

1. Preheat oven to 400 degrees.
2. In a large mixing bowl, mix the coconut flour with the salt and set aside.
3. In a separate mixing bowl, blend the butter, 1 tablespoon honey, and 2 eggs.
4. Add the wet ingredients to the dry and mix well.
5. Oil a 10 inch deep dish glass pie plate and press the crust mixture across the bottom and halfway up the sides of the pie dish. Bake 8 minutes.
6. Remove the crust and turn the oven down to 350 degrees.
7. Add the ½ cup honey, eggs, cream cheese, vanilla, and yogurt to a bowl and blend on low speed until smooth. Pour it into the pie crust and bake about 55 minutes.
8. Chill an hour or two before serving.

COOK'S NOTE
Using a glass or ceramic pie plate gives predictable results, but any pie plate can be used. The coconut flour crust will darken quite a bit and give it a nutty taste.

NUTRITIONAL INFORMATION
Calories 556 Carbohydrate 23g Fat 49g Protein 11g

BANANA NICE CREAM

Just one simple ingredient. Banana, with the look and taste of ice cream.

SERVES 2
INGREDIENTS

2 bananas, a bit overripe

1. Peel, cut into 4 chunks each, and freeze bananas in a freezer bag.
2. Add to a food processor and blend, occasionally stopping to scrape down the sides. The bananas transform into a creamy mix that resembles soft serve ice cream.

COOK'S NOTE

So many ingredients can be added for different flavors of ice cream. Some of my favorites are white chocolate, cherry jam, coconut milk or strawberries.

NUTRITIONAL INFORMATION
Calories 105 Carbohydrate 27g Fat .4g Protein 1g

CHERRY ICE CREAM

No ice cream maker is required for this simple antioxidant rich dessert.

SERVES 4
INGREDIENTS

2 cups vanilla whole milk yogurt
1 bag (12-16 ounces) frozen dark sweet cherries

1. Add the ingredients to a food processor and blend until smooth.
2. Transfer to a freezer-safe bowl, cover and freeze for 2 to 3 hours.

COOK'S NOTE

An optional addition to this ice cream can be melted vanilla chips. Simply add to the ingredients in the blender.

NUTRITIONAL INFORMATION
Calories 170 Carbohydrate 30g Fat 4.1g Protein 5g

WHITE CHOCOLATE CHIP COOKIES

America's favorite cookie made gluten-free with coconut flour and made low in oxalates by using white chocolate chips. A light textured cookie that is simple yet divine.

Makes 16-18
INGREDIENTS

¼ cup butter, melted
¼ cup honey
2 eggs
½ teaspoon vanilla
½ teaspoon baking soda
¼ teaspoon salt
½ cup coconut flour
¾ cup white chocolate chips

1. Preheat oven to 350 degrees.
2. Cover a large baking sheet with parchment paper.
3. In a medium-size bowl, mix the melted butter with the honey until smooth; then add in the eggs, vanilla, baking soda, and salt. Mix well.
4. Blend in the coconut flour and allow to stand for about 1 minute as the coconut flour absorbs the liquid ingredients. Then mix in the white chocolate chips.
5. Shape spoonfuls into balls and place on the baking sheet. Makes 16-18 cookies.
6. Using a fork, press down each cookie to the desired size. (Cookies will not spread out or rise much.)
7. Cook 15-16 minutes. The outside of the cookie should be a golden brown color.
8. Slide the parchment paper off onto a cooling rack and cool for 10 minutes before removing to a serving dish.

COOK'S NOTE

Using honey with coconut flour in a cookie recipe gives the perfect dough consistency for an excellent chewy cookie. These are a dream come true for the gluten intolerant and low-oxalate dieter.

NUTRITIONAL INFORMATION
Calories 293 Carbohydrate 22g Fat 22g Protein 4g

FRUITCAKE

This gluten-free fruitcake has a lighter texture but similar taste when compared to the traditional fruitcake.

SERVES 8-10
INGREDIENTS

7 tablespoons coconut flour
½ teaspoon baking soda
1 teaspoon baking powder
¼ teaspoon salt
1 teaspoon instant coffee grounds
6 tablespoons water
4 eggs
½ cup maple syrup
1 teaspoon vanilla
½ teaspoon nutmeg
¼ teaspoon ginger
½ cup coconut oil or ghee, melted
¼ cup unsweetened coconut, shredded
½ cup raisins
½ cup raw pumpkin seeds
½ cup dried pineapple, chopped
½ cup dried cherries, chopped

1. Preheat oven to 350 degrees.
2. Oil a 6x9 loaf pan.
3. Mix coconut flour, baking soda, baking powder, and salt in a medium-size bowl and set aside.
4. In a separate bowl, mix coffee and water first and then add in the eggs, syrup, vanilla, nutmeg, ginger, and coconut oil or ghee.
5. Pour the wet ingredients into the dry and mix well using an electric blender until very smooth. Stir in the shredded coconut, raisins, pumpkin seeds, pineapple, and cherries and pour the mix into the baking dish.
6. Bake 40 minutes.
7. Allow to cool before removing from pan.

COOK'S NOTE
Fruitcake dates back to the middle ages. Recipes have varied greatly throughout the ages depending on what was available. This variation replaces grain flour with coconut flour and eliminates the alcohol which was

traditionally used to preserve the fruitcake. Fruitcakes are enjoyed throughout the year in most countries today, but in the US, it's mainly served during the Christmas holidays. However, this tasty variation may have you preparing it throughout the year.

* Some brands of baking powder use wheat starch to absorb moisture. Rumford and Clabber Girl brands are wheat free and aluminum free as well.

NUTRITIONAL INFORMATION
Calories 266 Carbohydrate 23g Fat 18.3g Protein 5g

LEMON PUDDING
Slightly tart but with an amazing smoothness.

SERVES 4
INGREDIENTS

½ cup coconut milk
⅔ cup lemon juice
½ cup cottage cheese
2 tablespoons cornstarch
¼ cup honey
¼ teaspoon salt

1. Add all of the ingredients to a blender and process until smooth.
2. Pour into a saucepan and bring to a boil over medium heat.
3. Allow to cool. Then pour into 4 glasses or bowls and refrigerate at least 2 hours.
4. Serve chilled.

COOK'S NOTE
The taste is very similar to a combination of lemon icebox pie and cheesecake.

NUTRITIONAL INFORMATION
Calories 183 Carbohydrate 26g Fat 8.4g Protein 4g

RICE PUDDING

A wholesome, heartwarming dessert with a creamy vanilla base.

SERVES 4
INGREDIENTS

1 ½ cups white rice, cooked
2 cups milk or coconut milk, divided
¼ cup honey
½ teaspoon salt
1 egg
1 tablespoon butter
½ teaspoon vanilla
¼ teaspoon nutmeg

1. Mix the cooked rice, 1 ½ cups milk, honey and salt. Cook uncovered over medium heat for about 15-20 minutes.
2. Whisk egg and remaining milk in a bowl.
3. Add about 1 cup of the hot rice mixture to the egg while stirring. Add it back to the pan and cook 2 minutes more.
4. Remove from the heat and add the butter, vanilla, and nutmeg.
5. Serve warm.

COOK'S NOTE

When made with natural ingredients, rice pudding can be a healthier alternative to other deserts.

NUTRITION INFORMATION
Calories 304 Carbohydrate 58g Fat 5g Protein 7g

WHITE CHOCOLATE CHERRY SQUARES

A simple yet elegant looking dessert of chewy cherries in sweet white chocolate.

SERVES 8-10
INGREDIENTS

1/3 cup coconut oil or butter, melted
2 cups white chocolate chips
1 ½ teaspoons vanilla
A pinch of salt
1 cup dried cherries

1. In a medium-size saucepan, melt the coconut oil or butter and chocolate chips over medium-high heat stirring constantly.
2. Remove from heat and blend in the vanilla, salt, and cherries.
3. Pour into an oiled 9x13 glass baking dish.
4. Refrigerate for about an hour before cutting and serving.

COOK'S NOTE

Continually dip a sharp knife in a glass of hot water to cut the squares. Cherries are packed with antioxidants and offer many health benefits.

NUTRITIONAL INFORMATION
Calories 314 Carbohydrate 2 g Fat 23g Protein 3g

SUNBUTTER OAT COOKIES

An easy gluten-free recipe for flourless, healthy, filling oatmeal cookies.

SERVES 4-6
INGREDIENTS

1 egg
1 cup sunbutter
½ cup honey
⅔ cup oats
1 teaspoon baking soda
¼ teaspoon salt

1. Preheat oven to 350 degrees.
2. In a medium-size bowl whisk the egg, and then add the remaining ingredients.
3. Chill the dough for 30 minutes.
4. Preheat the oven to 350 degrees.
5. Shape spoonfuls into balls (about 12) and place on a parchment paper lined baking sheet. Using a fork, press down to flatten into cookie size.
6. Bake 8 minutes. It's very important not to overbake the cookies. The cookies will look very soft and undercooked.
7. Allow the cookies to cool for 10 minutes on the baking sheet before transferring to a wire rack to cool completely.

COOK'S NOTE

Sometimes, but not always, the natural chlorophyll in sunflower seeds reacts with baking soda, causing a green color inside the cookies after they cool. This is completely harmless! Sunbutter is peanut-free, tree-nut free, and gluten-free, so it's great for people with these types of food allergies. It also has 1/3 less saturated fat than peanut butter and 27 percent of your daily recommended allowance of Vitamin E in one serving.

NUTRITIONAL INFORMATION
Calories 476 Carbohydrate 49g Fat 31.1g Protein 13g

RECIPE INDEX

Breakfasts, Brunches and Breads

Soups, Salads and Dressings

Side Dishes

Main Dishes

Snacks and Sweets

ABOUT THE AUTHOR

Melinda Keen, B.S., CNC, is an author and educator. Her first cookbook, *Low Oxalate Fresh and Fast Cookbook* (2015) grew out of her desire to help others prepare a variety of fresh and healthy low-oxalate meals. Her second cookbook, *Real Food Real Results* (2016) includes gluten-free, low-oxalate, and nutrient-rich recipes. *Living Low Oxalate* (2018) is a resource book that reveals how oxalate rich foods are linked to bladder pain, kidney stones, joint pain and inflammation, chronic fatigue, and fibromyalgia. This well researched, easy-to-read book explains what oxalates are, which foods contain this natural toxin and how they can adversely affect your health.

Printed in Great Britain
by Amazon

16537123R00104